Great Spaces

Flexible Homes

Edition 2006

Author: Arian Mostaedi

Publisher: Carles Broto

Editorial Coordinator: Jacobo Krauel

Graphic designer & production: Dimitris Kottas

Text: contributed by the architects, edited by William George

© Carles Broto i Comerma

Jonqueres, 10, 1-5

08003 Barcelona, Spain

Tel.: +34 93 301 21 99

 Fax: +34-93-301 00 21

E-mail: info@linksbooks.net

www. linksbooks.net

Great Spaces

Flexible Homes

LINKS

index

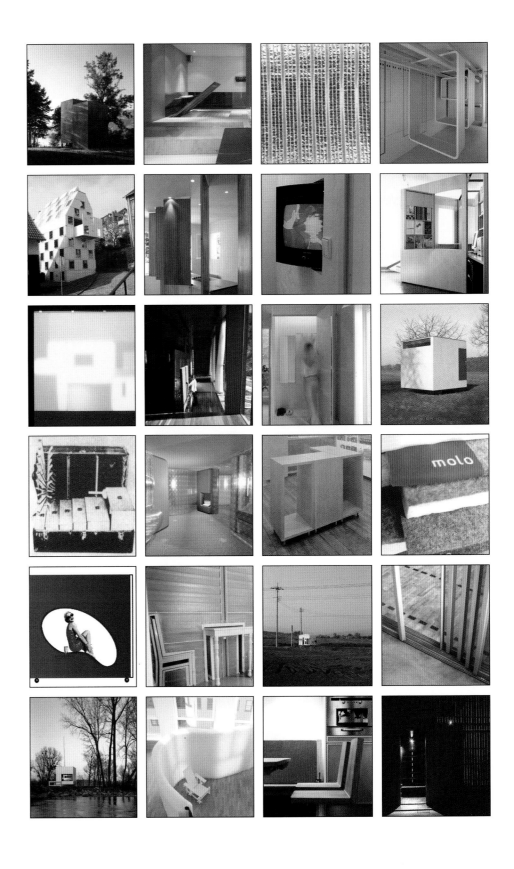

introduction

Right now, constructive alternatives are on the drawing board or being built all over the world, which share an important characteristic: flexibility. As a crucial subject within contemporary architecture, this book gathers the most significant examples of it.

A wide range of different starting points is manifest, from sociological experiments to aesthetic questioning. The achievement, along the way, is the maximum utilization of available space, creatively using the most advanced technology.

Geographically distant cultures come into contact, and different ways of living and being exert a reciprocal influence. Our mobile, dynamic society, in a constant state of evolution, has spawned a generation of designers whose projects brazenly address the future while deeply interrogating our own nature. Parallel lines of research are generated by social, economic and environmental factors, interacting together in the present: important factors are the value of urban space, a changing model of the family unit and the new urban dweller, prototypically nomadic and self employed. Equally important is the desire to avoid our lives being determined by the rigid mold of the space we inhabit. These pages contain projects of a private and of a public nature, some designed for work, others for leisure, or combining it all. Some resolve definite problems in innovative ways; others, more experimentally, take the possibilities of a viable living space to the limit, within the context of a computerized society. All of them address the borderlines between technology and art, between a dwelling machine and the aesthetic object, with a refreshing brand of humor and imagination.

Each project is fully represented in color photographs that convey relevant information and a precise idea of its aspect. Floor plans, elevations, and diagrams of important details, illustrate the valuable explanations given by the building's authors. As a creative stimulus, this book offers a key to some of the most inspiring architecture now and in the immediate future.

Photographs:
Paul Ott

Gucklhupf

Lake Mondsee, Austria

Its name combines that of a nearby hill (Guglhupf), an Austrian cake (Gucklhupf), and the verbs gucken and hüpfen (Gucken: to watch, Hüpfen: to hop), hopping up and down to see. The Gucklhupf emerged as one of the cultural, artistic and architectural events within the 1993 Festival of the Regions, in northern Austria.

During the summer, workshops, on-site interventions, musical spectacles, etc. dealt with "strangeness" as a main theme. Wörndl used his cousin's plot of land beside the Mondsee lake, for his interpretation of the festival's idea by means of a constructed object expressive of the tension between opposites – strange versus familiar, still versus moving, habitation versus travel, home versus away –.

The Gucklhupf is an experimental home consisting of three assembled squares, built of enameled marine plywood (4 x 6 x 7 m), on a very basic structure of studs (12 x 12 cm) and beams (6 x 12 cm) to carry the outer fiber-board cladding. Automatic devices and retractable panels at various heights are joined to the structure with dowels, flaps and stainless steel cables. In the interior, two levels and a half cover a surface of 48 m².

The pavilion was built by Wörndl himself with two assistants, according to a variable plan, with details decided as the work-in-progress developed. The purpose was to create a live object, potentially in a state of permanent change. During the six-week festival it was used as a contemplative space, a stage for musical performances or poetry readings; the rest of the year the building was used for country weekends, sun bathing, or temporary shelter. In the winter it is a boathouse.

Despite the initial approval of the structure as a permanent exhibition space and sculptural element, the authorities were pressured by the public to rule its removal. The fate of the Gucklhupf was finally decided in the administrative tribunal. Although a neighboring community offered an alternative site, the Gucklhupf was finally left to the care of the truck drivers from the construction company. It is now disassembled, waiting for a chance to be reconstructed.

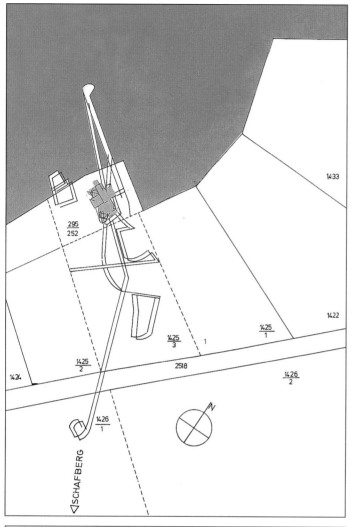

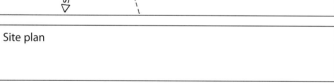

Site plan

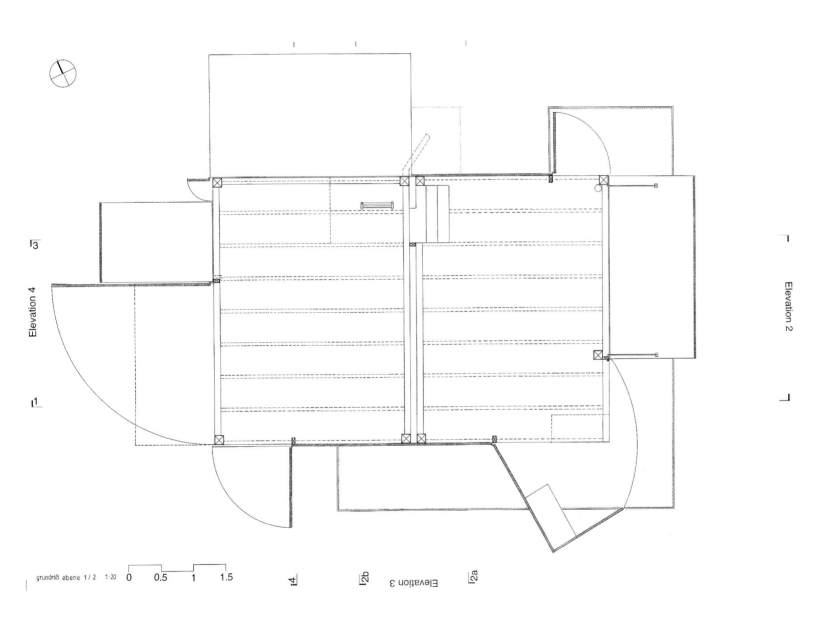

Elevation 3

Elevation 4

Elevation 2

grundriß ebene 1 / 2   1:20   0   0.5   1   1.5

Ground floor plan

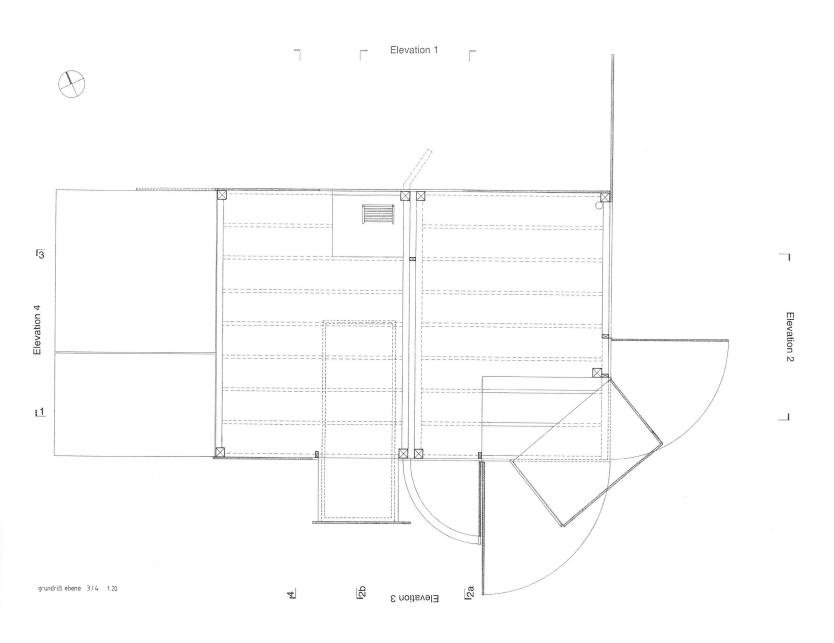

Elevation 1

Elevation 4

Elevation 2

3

1

grundriß ebene 3 / 4 1.20

Elevation 3

4

2b

2a

First floor plan

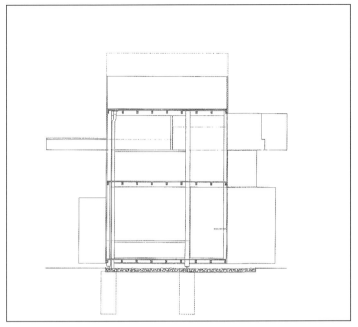

Section 2a

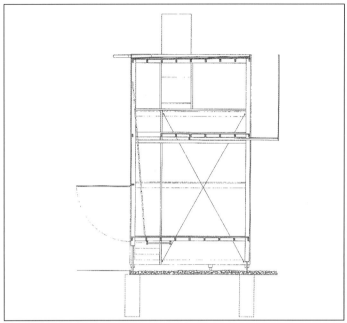

Section 2b

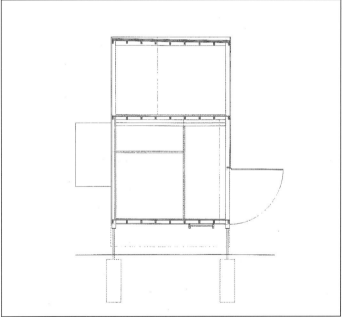

Section 4

14

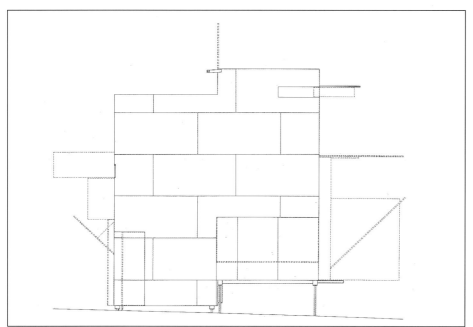

Elevation 1

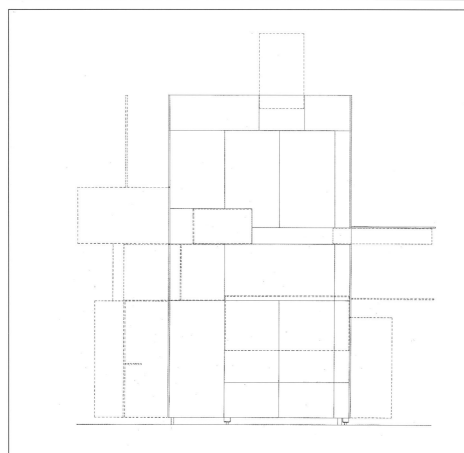

Elevation 2

Elevation 3

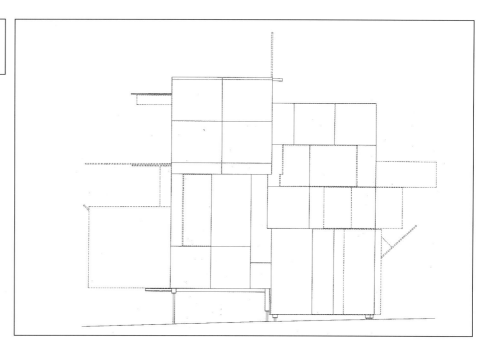

Elevation 4

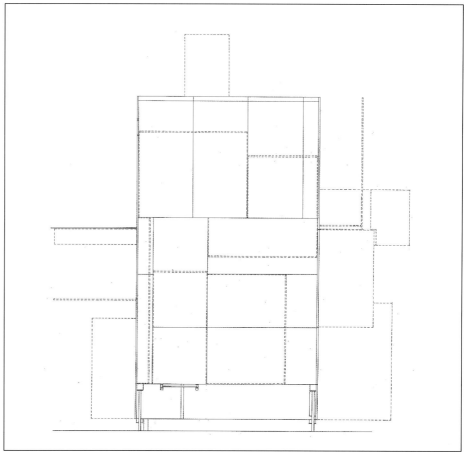

Johnson Chou

Photographs:
Volker Seding

Womb: **w**ork, **o**ffice, **m**editation, **b**ase

Toronto, Canada

'Retreat' invokes more than escape – we retreat to contemplate, reflect and create, to harness the creativity and focus we sometimes lack. It is where we physically and intellectually rejuvenate, a place where books are written, design concepts formed - where one is creatively inspired.

A multi-functional (home/office) space, Womb (for work, office, meditation, base), recognizes that our refuge must fulfill a variety of needs. Designed to be four rooms in one, the space transforms as desired, maintaining an elementally ethereal aesthetic.

With furniture and cabinetry that pivot and disappear into walls and floors with a touch of a button, Womb offers four programmatic rooms that occupy the entire 600sqft (56m^2) space; kitchen/dining, work/office, bedroom/living, spa/bath, all within a spare, Zen-like meditative environment. Womb proposes a 21st century 'machine for living' – concealing what isn't immediately necessary, eliminating visual distractions and quadrupling its spatial effectiveness.

The kitchen unit slides into the wall when not needed, and the empty space allows a table to pivot around, a clean work area with an unobstructed view across the pool to the exterior. Sink and work surfaces are hidden under covers that open to an upright position. In the center of the room, the bathing/reflecting pool and suspended stainless steel fireplace anchor the space as the only fixed elements.

Expanding and contracting as needed, the washroom is situated centrally near the pool and fireplace. A "u"-shaped wall that conceals the bathroom slides to allow one to enter, or to enclose the occupant for privacy. When not in use, the wall automatically closes, completely regaining the space. The living area, separated by the pool from the work/kitchen space, contains a bed that disappears into the floor when not required, allowing a cantilevered couch to fold out from the wall.

The walls are a blank canvas for lighting to transform, fluorescents creating a cool white daytime space that recessed halogen lights turn to a warmer intimacy by evening. Further modulation is achieved with fiber-optics that "paint" the walls with variable hues.

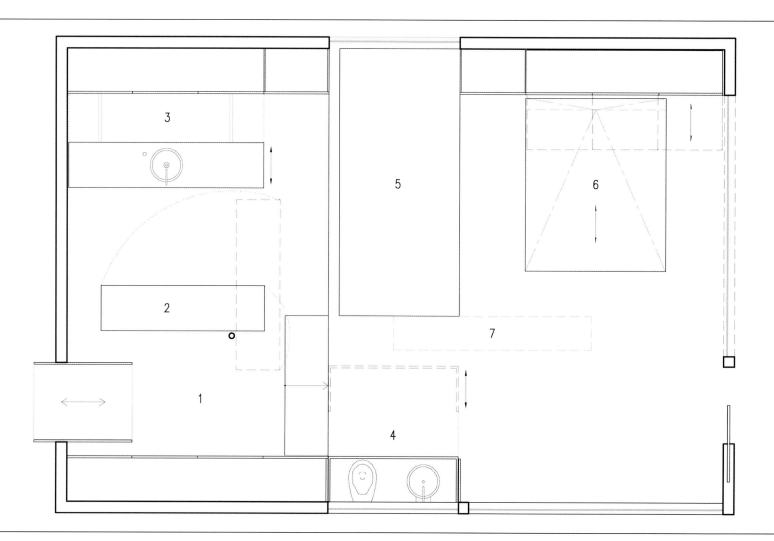

1. Foyer
2. Pivoting table
3. Retractable kitchen
4. Bathroom
5. Whirlpool/bath
6. Bedroom
7. Fireplace

Animated by the ballet movements of the architectural elements, bathed in nuances of light, this is an environment designed to inspire reflection, creation and contemplation yet able to transform itself for living purposes. Womb is truly a base for work, office and meditation.

Kalhöfer - Korschildgen

Photographs:
Christèle Jany,
Wilfried Dechau

Fahrt Ins Grüne

Lüttringhausen, Germany

The clients inhabit the ground floor of a typical timber-frame house with a large garden, located in a nature reserve. They needed a study added. The much-used garden was only accessible from the basement via an internal staircase. Direct access to the garden was not required as the extension was temporary: shared use of the first floor was planned. As the terrace was used during the summer, the extension should be removable at that time of year. The space should have immediate access from the house during the winter.

The aims were:

- Stronger integration of the house and the garden.

- Different summer and winter use.

- The extension should admit a different function when shared use of the first floor begins (it will probably become a greenhouse).

The new part mimics an existing extension added in the 1950s. The distinction is established by the materials. The main supporting structure is a steel frame. The exterior is clad with transparent, rigid corrugated PVC panels. The inner skin is a simple timber frame construction with thermal insulation between plywood panels. A nylon-reinforced reflective sheet is applied on the outer panel to prevent the interior from overheating. This low-budget construction can be easily removed in case of functional change.

The surfaces reflect the surroundings and the changing daylight conditions. The cavity behind the transparent PVC houses the technical equipment (telecommunication, electricity), visible outside like an exposed neural network. Despite the rough industrially manufactured materials the layering of inner and outer skin evokes a poetic depth.

Daylight enters through the window, the glass door and the skylight. The terrace floor is a metal grate that lets light into the space below. The terrace railings are easily removed. The sliding mechanism consists of industrial heavy-duty runners in steel channel tracks.

Various different spaces evolved besides the created interior space and the terrace. They are subject to constant changes determined by the path of the sun, artificial illumination and last but not least the mobility of the extension.

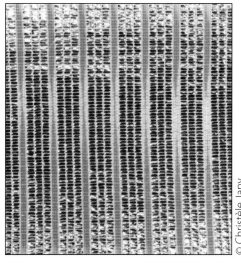

© Christèle Jany

26

27

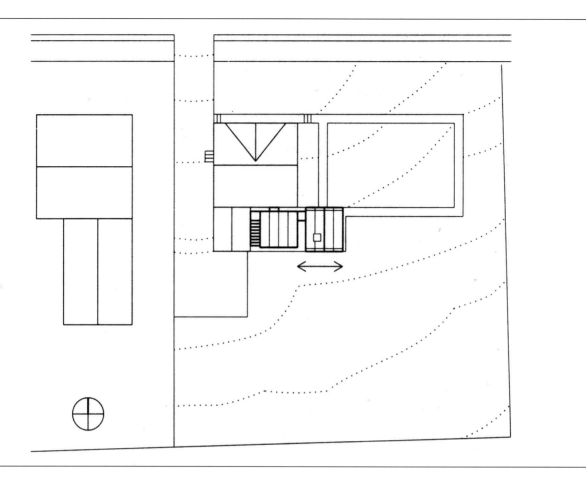

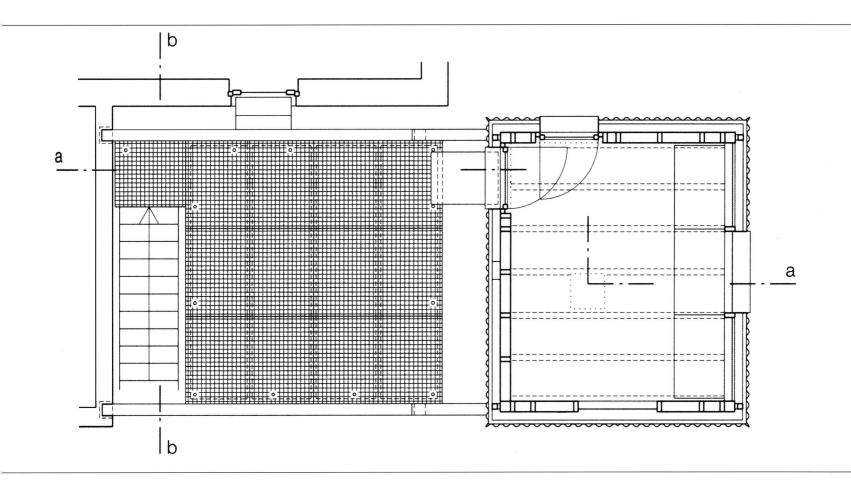

29

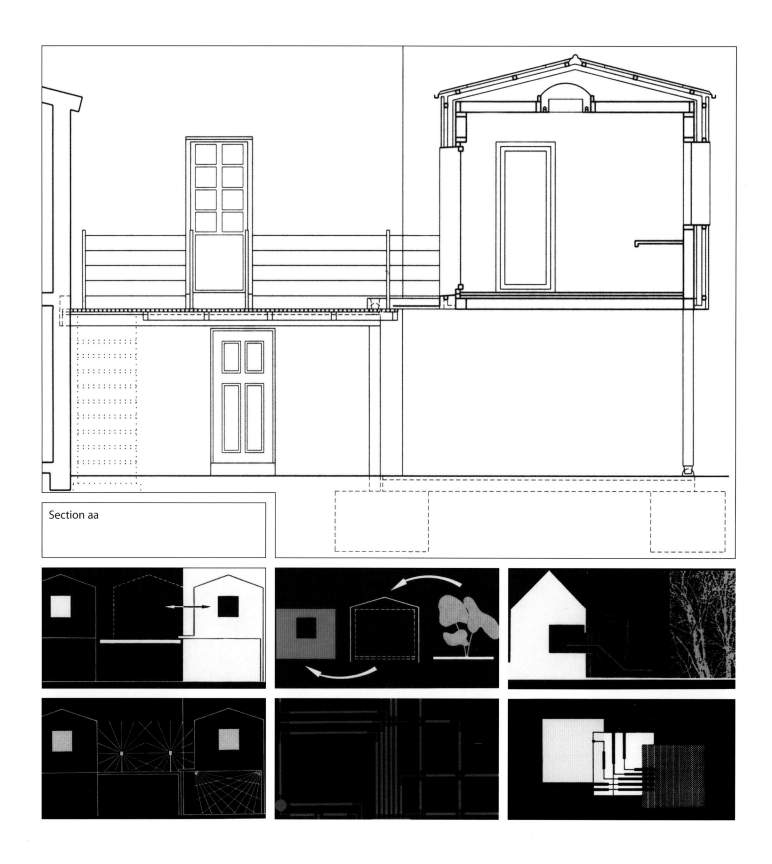

Section aa

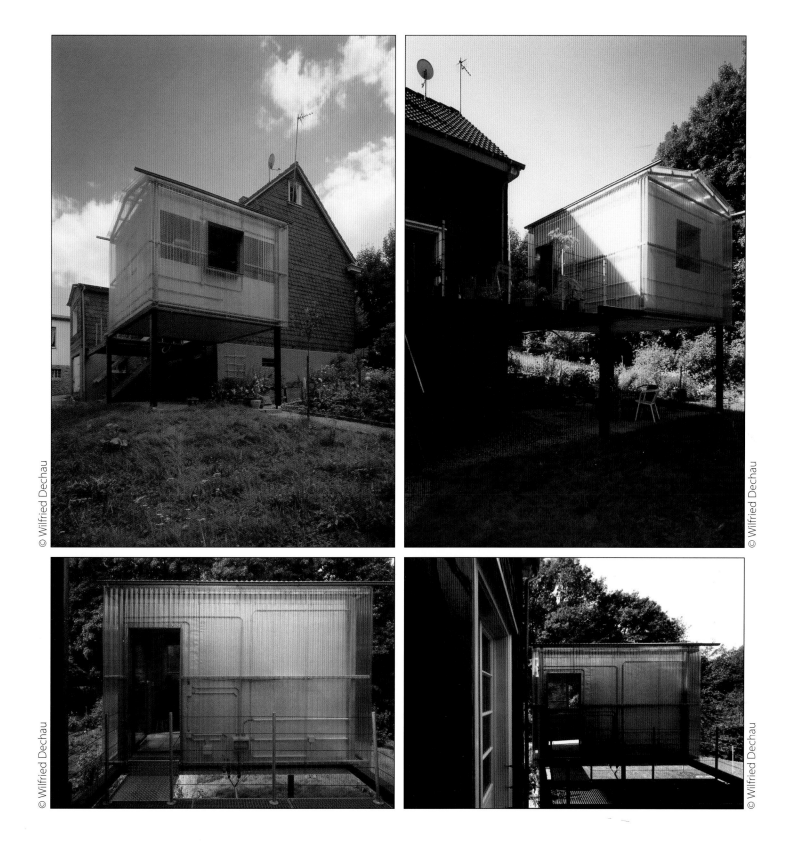

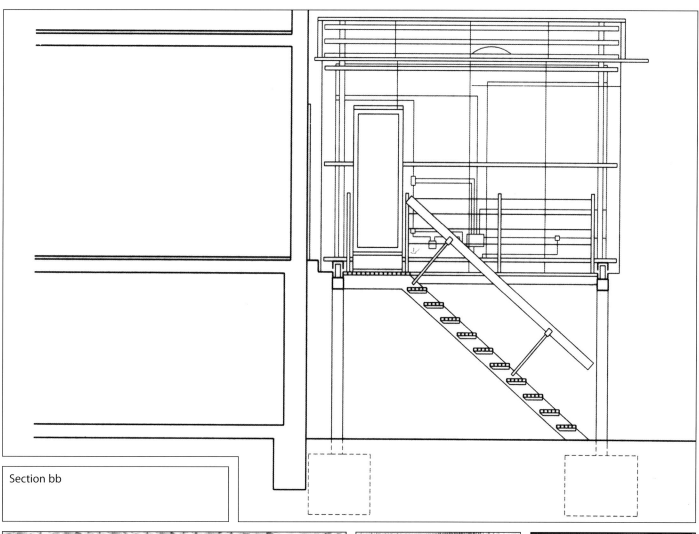

Section bb

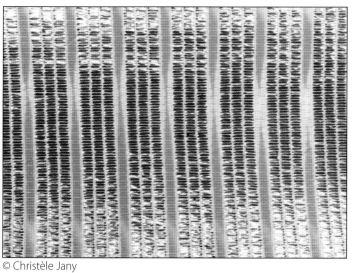

© Christèle Jany

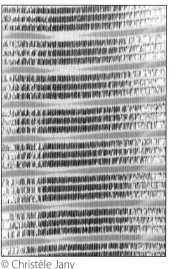

© Christèle Jany

© Wilfried Dechau

DETAIL OF THE RUNNER IN THE TRACK

A- Summer position:
Floor extension, terrace.
B- Winter position:
Connection to house.

1. Concrete stone tiles 40 mm
2. Aluminum sheet 4 mm
3. Square steel structural tube 50/50/4 mm
4. Square steel structural tube 150/150 mm
5. Steel grating 30 mm
6. Square steel structural tube 110/60/5.6 mm
7. U shaped steel track for roller
8. Insect screen
9. Metal break, 12 mm, for track
10. Zincified round steel tubing ø38/4 mm
11. Zincified footplate ø110/3.2 mm
12. Zincified baseplate ø65/3.2 mm
13. Reversible synthetic keel d=5 mm

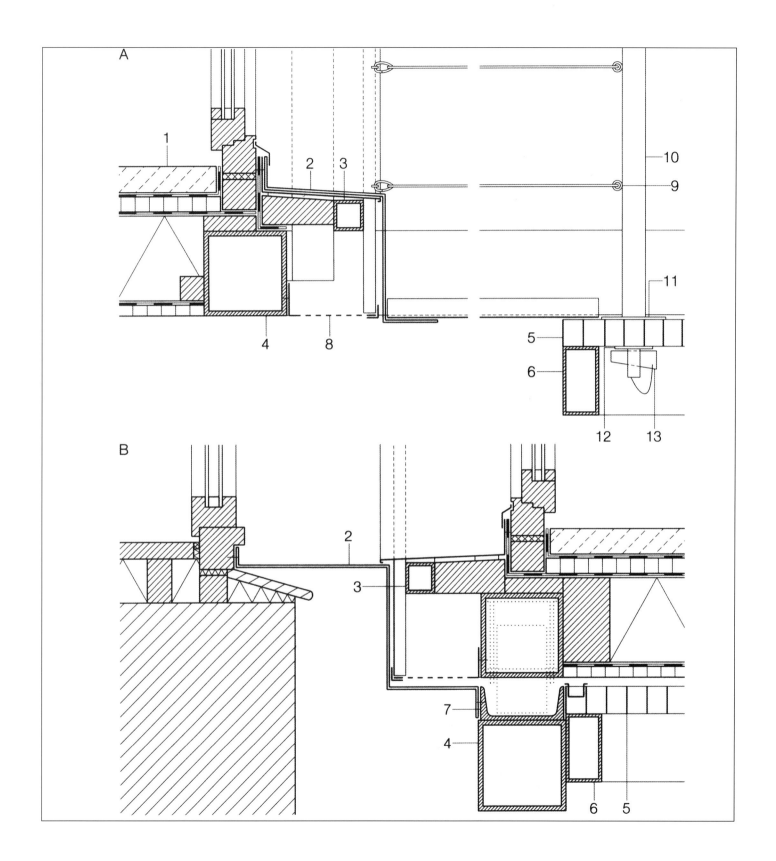

CircuitBox

Odaiba, Tokyo, Japan

For the Italian presence at the Tokyo Design Week 2004, the Italian Trade Commission organized a national competition entitled "Open Living in Container". The competition brief asked young architects, designers and artists to imagine an installation illustrative of the evolution of the "Italian Living" adapted to the limited space of a shipping container. A jury of well-know architects, designers, design critics and journalists from Italy and Japan selected "CircuitBox"0, by Studio X Design Group, as the first prize winner and the project has been built inside the "Container Ground Exhibition" at Odaiba, Tokyo.

The shrinking size of habitation units and a freer concept of domestic environments have led to spatial integration and an increasing demand for flexibility. Thus the living room is no longer one room in a house but has become the house itself, incorporating a variety of functions. To permit mixed usage, a single space for a life style without barriers demands versatility, requiring the space to turn from private to public and vice versa several times a day.

With a not so distant future in mind, Studio X Design Group developed a system of multifunctional furnishings they called CircuitBox. It is a compact living unit with all the necessary elements in a minimal space, which can be plugged in like an electric circuit.

CircuitBox consists of a series of rings of gradually decreasing size, fitted one inside the other like a Russian doll. The largest ring should be anchored to a wall as it contains fixed services like the kitchen and the bath, as well as being the container of all the other rings. The consecutively smaller rings are movable, hanging from a rail which they slide along, passing one through the other. Each one of them may be equipped with a set of accessories to meet the user's needs, defining each ring's function and the function of the room when a particular ring is presiding over the space. Extracting, placing and arranging the rings adequately, the ambience can be transformed from dining room to office, bedroom, or anything else in answer to the needs of living in the already present future.

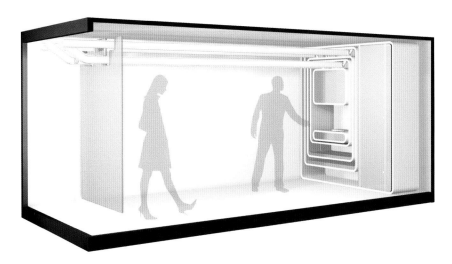

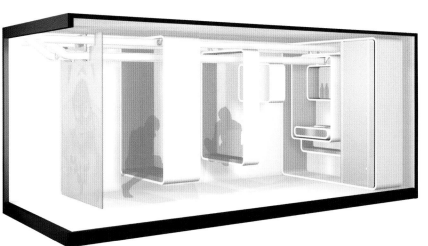

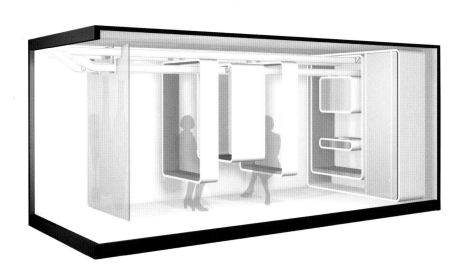

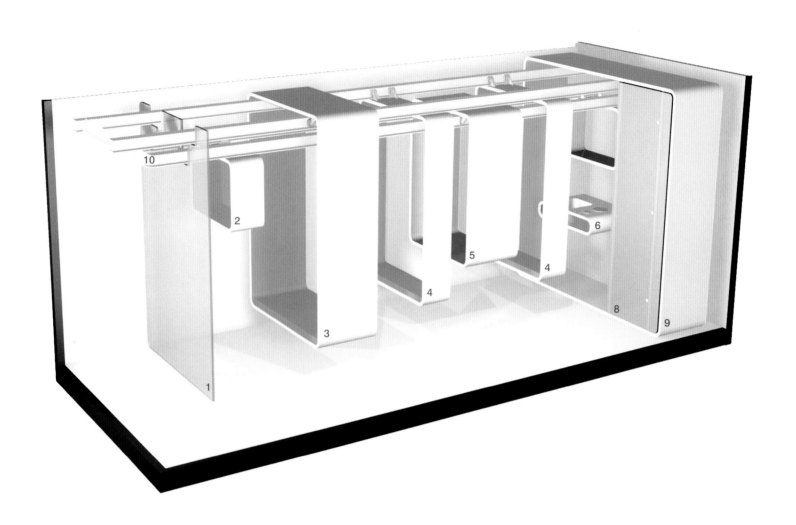

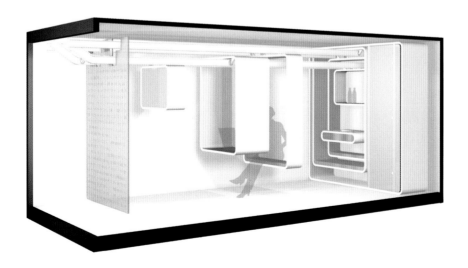

1. Translucent projector screen
2. Media shelf
3. Sofa
4. Chair
5. Table
6. Kitchen
7. Shelf
8. Bathroom
9. External ring
10. Slide support

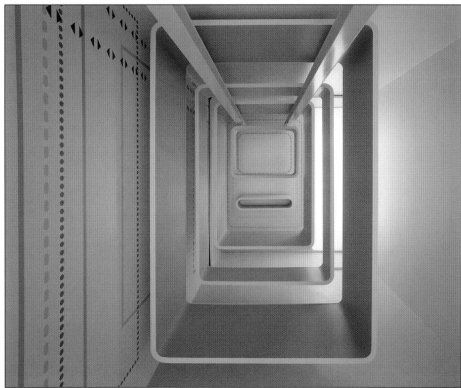

CircuitBox consists of a series of rings of gradually decreasing size, fitted one inside the other like a Russian doll. The largest ring should be anchored to a wall as it contains fixed services like the kitchen and the bath, as well as being the container of all the other rings. The consecutively smaller rings are movable, hanging from a rail which they slide along, passing one through the other. Each one of them may be equipped with a set of accessories to meet the user's needs, defining each ring's function and the function of the room when a particular ring is presiding over the space. Extracting, placing and arranging the rings adequately, the ambience can be transformed from dining room to office, bedroom, or anything else in answer to the needs of living in the already present future.

Seifert + Stöckmann

Photographs:
Juergen Holzenleuchter,
Seifert + Stöckmann

Living room

Gelnhausen, Germany

The old house at no.15 Kuhgasse, Gelnhausen, probably built soon after the Thirty Years war, was never a fine building, yet the architect's bought it. In accordance with conservation ruling, the new design replicated the volume and geometry of the old building - but everything else was different. The small house needed a sense of largeness, so a single room was made, extending from the floor to the gable, from one external wall to the other. Openness was wanted – inside-out and vice versa – so a rigorous grid of windows enveloped the walls and the roof, with battlements added to the gable. To connect with the earth the interior was designed around a large boulder.

All service areas are small and incorporated into a hollow gable wall. A box suspended between the gable walls contains the private spaces. The high deck has the fireplace and views of the town, moon and sky.

The house should have an independent form within the context of the historic town. Neither alien nor familiar; respectful of the locale, but typologically cleaner. The elevations have been ordered and the material has been unified: roof and wall, outside and inside. A house as a membrane between interior and exterior.

Underlining this, part of the front gable wall can slide out into space like a drawer and becomes a balcony.

During the planning phase artists were invited to develop works for the house, particularly artists with different concepts of art in society. Some favour the autonomy of art, others use their work to intervene in everyday life and social processes. The artwork in the Kuhgasse derive from the artists' own sensibilities, a collection of individual standpoints, with no overriding content, only the house in common – the shared circumstance of their conception.

Combining traces of the old house, landscape, lyrics, painting, sculpture, architecture, prose, sound and light, a context may emerge, an open station for different artistic, architectural and poetic positions.

Everything is oriented inwards as well as outwards, but not in a representative way. The house stands for itself and awaits response.

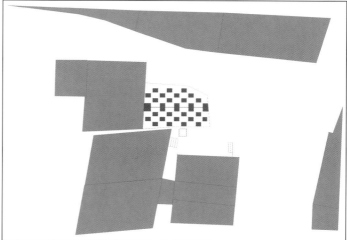

The house should have an independent form within the context of the historic town. Neither alien nor familiar; respectful of the locale, but typologically cleaner. The elevations have been ordered and the material has been unifyed: roof and wall, outside and inside. The almost model-like house hides its constructive details: no rooftiles, no gutters, the same all-over pervasive rhythm; closed surfaces for art installations, open surfaces for light and views. No tectonics, no legible stories, but an overplayed entrance. A house as a membrane between interior and exterior.

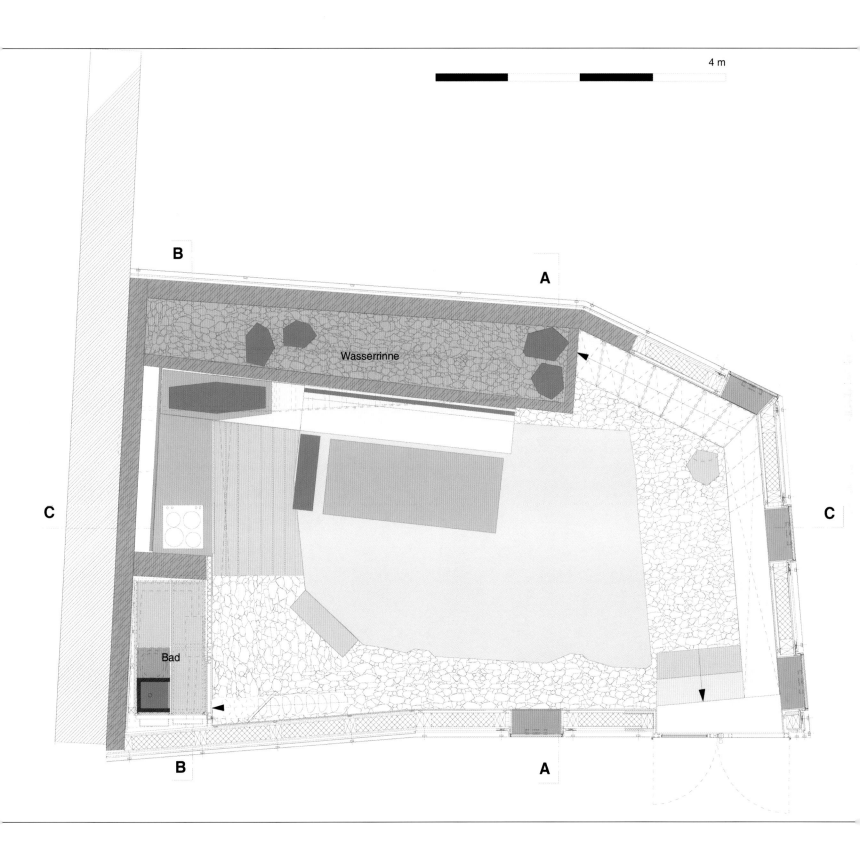

4 m

B

A

Wasserrinne

C

C

Bad

B

A

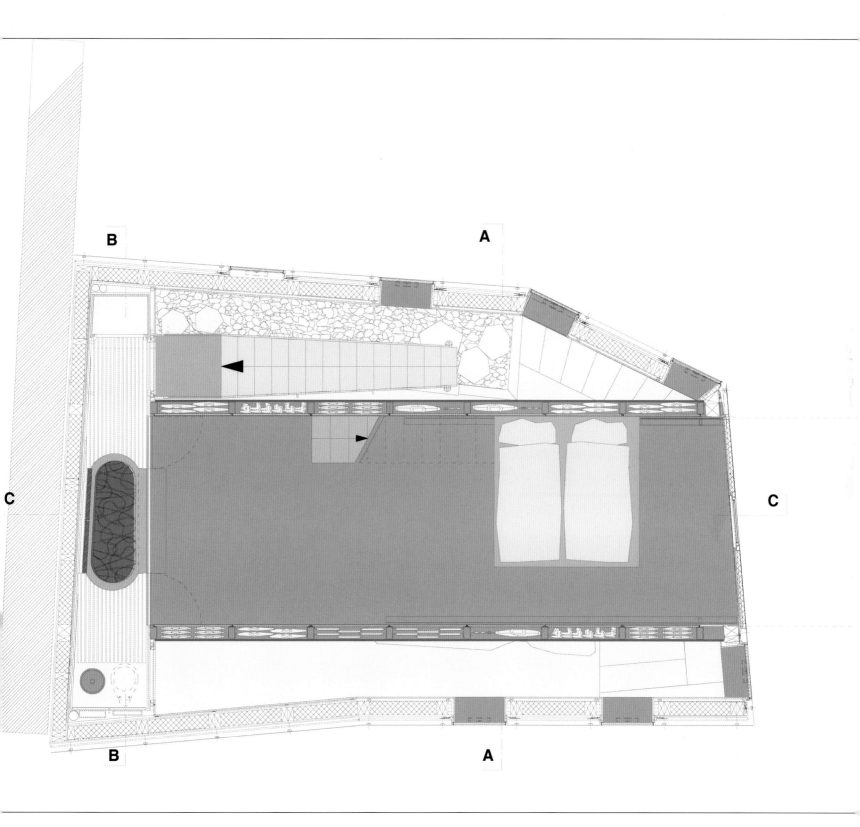

The old house at no.15 Kuhgasse, Gelnhausen, problably built soon after the Thirty Years war, was never a fine building, yet the architect's bought it. The old town is a conservation area with landmarks including Friedrich Barbarossa's Staufer palace, but the conservation department and structural engineers found nothing that would warrant its restoration. So finally, it was decided to demolish it and build something new. In accordance with conservation ruling, the new design replicated the volume and geometry of the old building - but everything else was different.

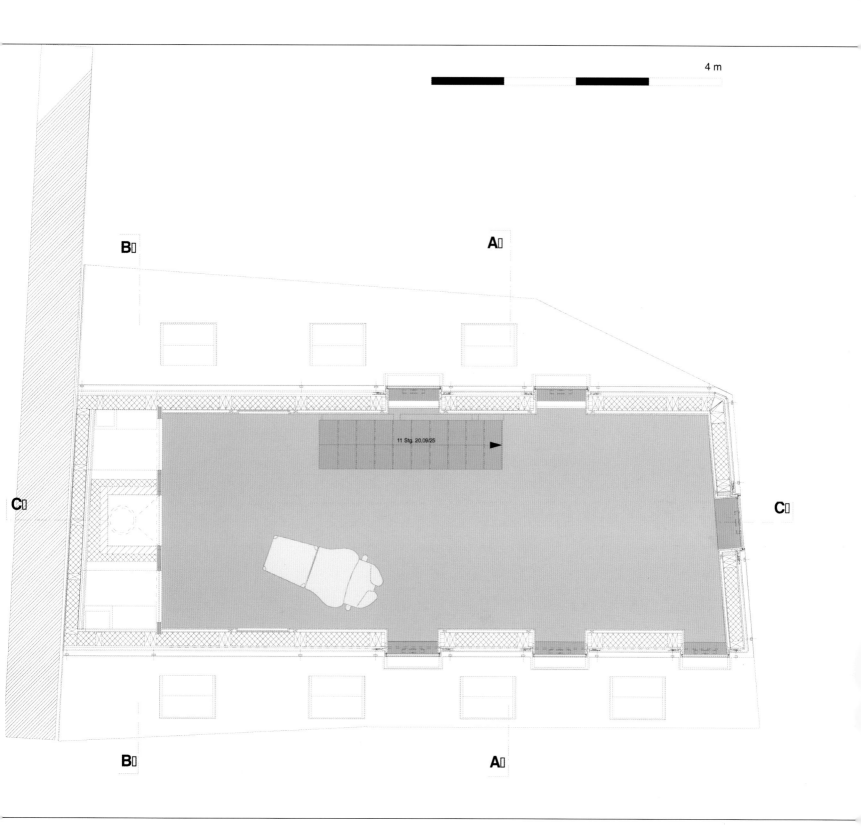

B◻   A◻

C◻   C◻

B◻   A◻

11 Stg. 20,09/25

4 m

49

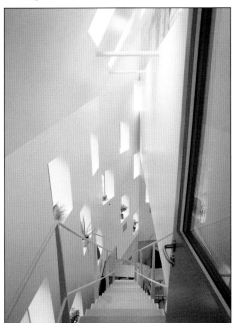

noise noise noise noise noise noise
ise noise noise noise noise noise noise
e noise noise noise noise noise noise noise
noise noise noise noise noise
se noise noise noise noise noise
oise noise noise noise noise
ise noise noise noise noise noise
noise noi noise nois
ise noise se noise
e noise n   sound   noise no   sound   se noise noise n   sound
noise noi noise noi
ise noise se noise
noise noi ise noise
noise noi noise noise
ise noise noise noise noise noise
noise noise noise noise noise noise
ise noise noise noise noise noise

sound: sonido   noise: ruido

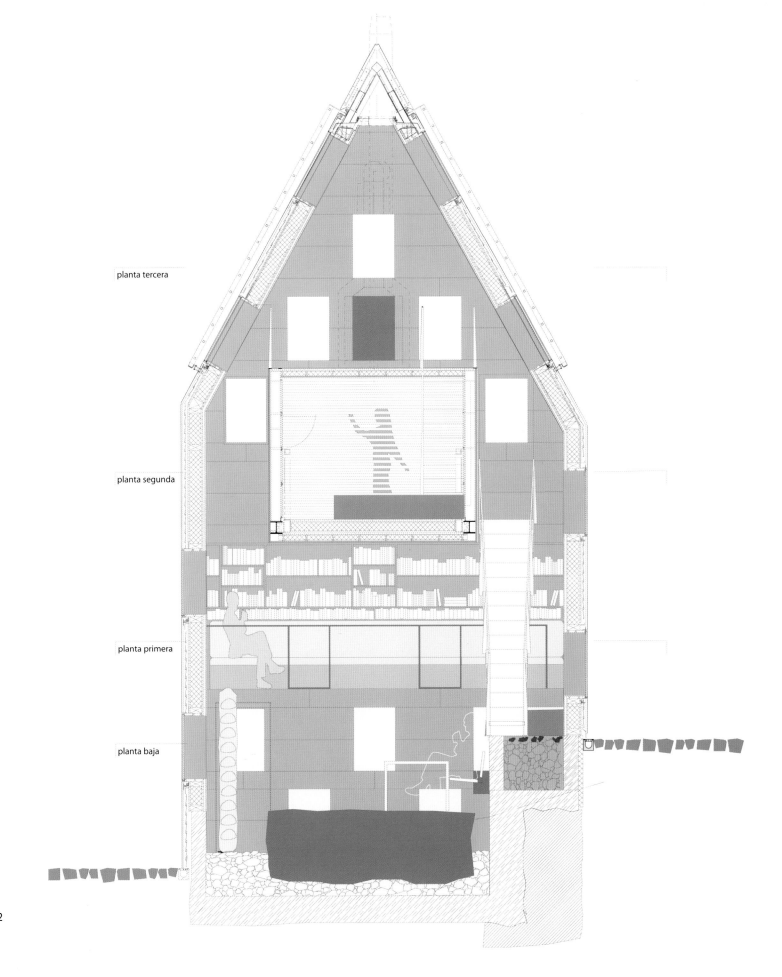

planta tercera

planta segunda

planta primera

planta baja

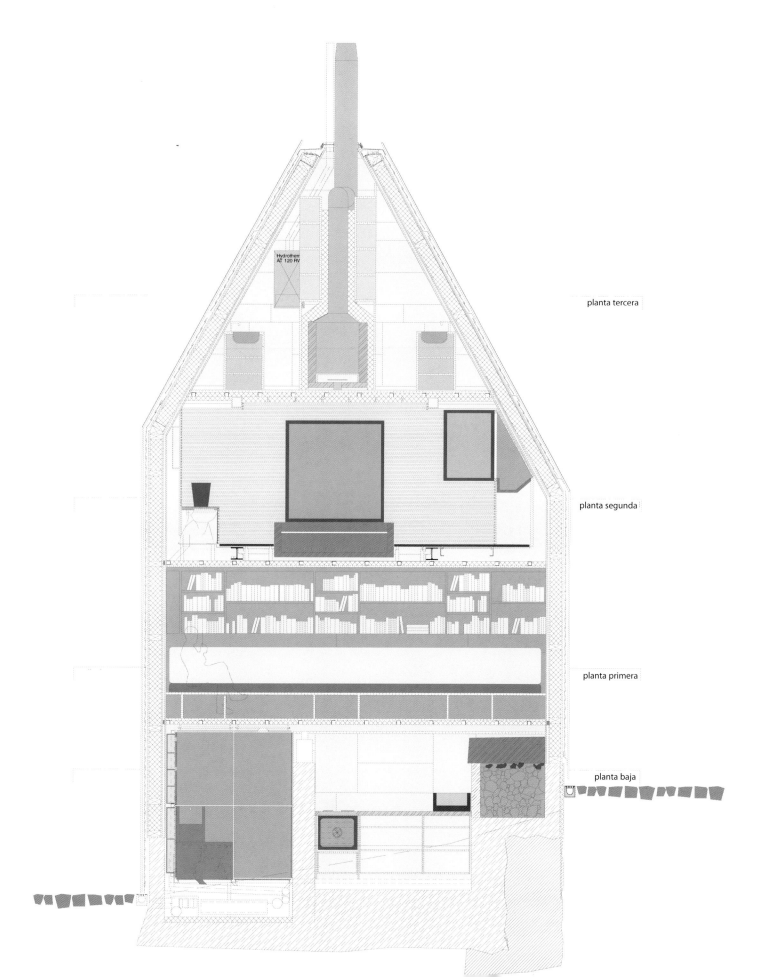

planta tercera

planta segunda

planta primera

planta baja

53

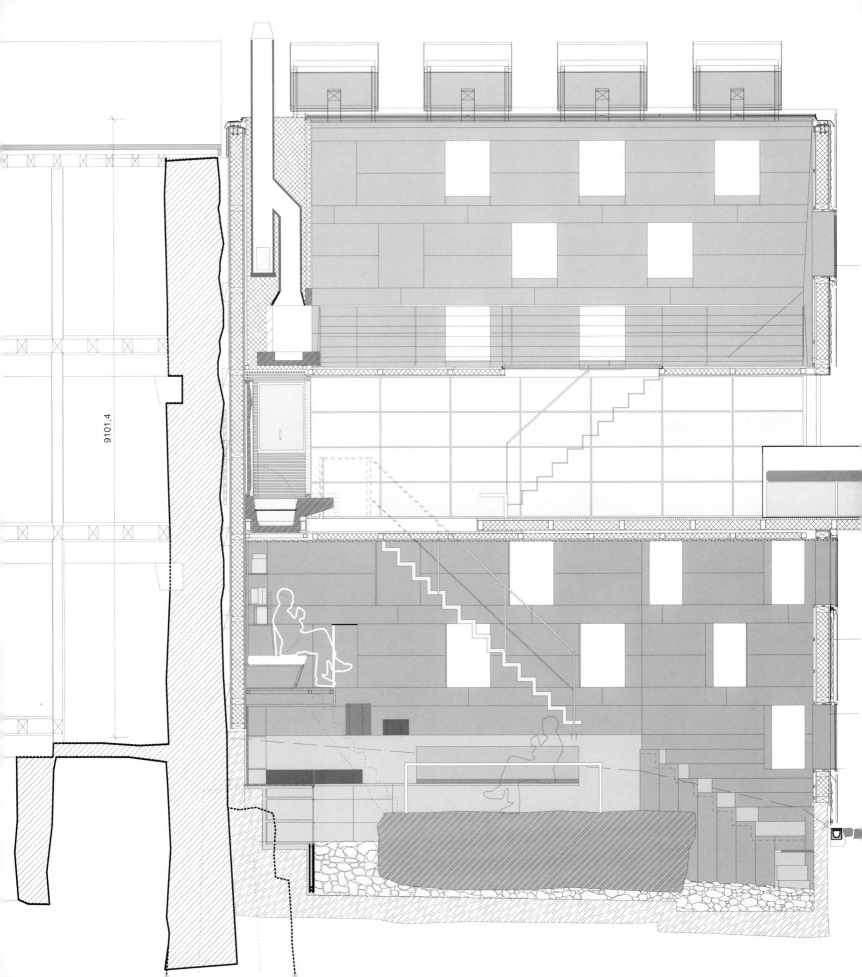

9101.4

Photographs:
Contributed by the architects

Villa les Roses

Aix-en-Provence, France

This dwelling, built in the fifties, is an inhabitable pavilion of 60 sqm located at the entrance to a forest in the north-west of Aix-en-Provence that has been declared a protected area. As the regulations of the area only permitted the construction of 30% of the plot, the old garage had to be rehabilitated and enlarged to respond to the new needs of the clients, a couple with two children.

The dwelling has a living room, kitchen, bathroom, scullery, office and two bedrooms. This scheme thus responds to two seemingly contradictory requirements: to allow each room to work independently without this being a nuisance, and to maintain a large fluidity between the spaces.

The distribution of the functional programme is governed by two perpendicular elements that allow the space to be occupied. The first element consists of a technical block housing the kitchen, the scullery, a toilet and a bathroom. The second element is formed by a functional block housing the cupboards, a mobile partition and an office. The doors and woodwork were made in okume plywood.

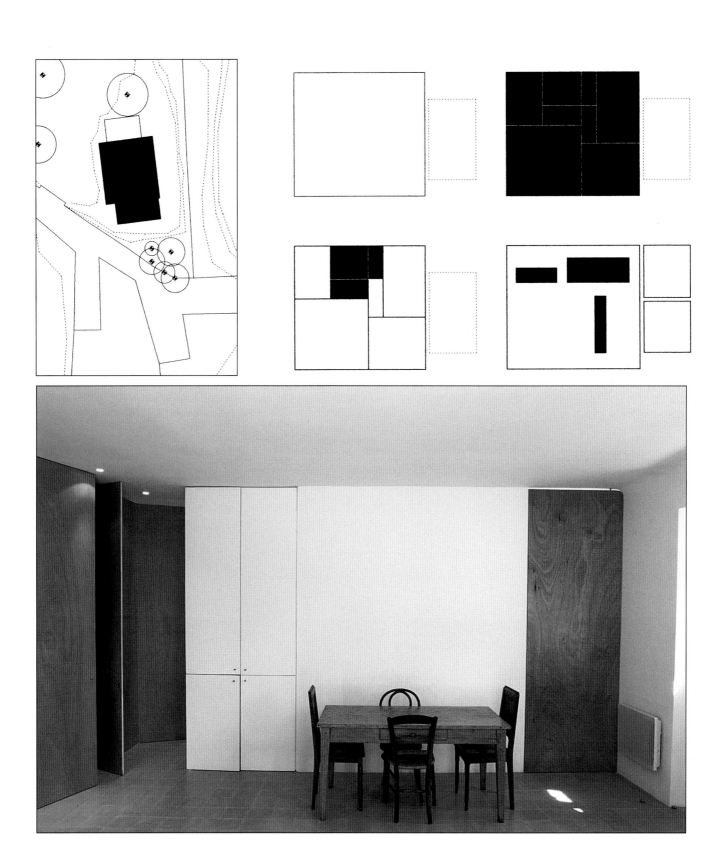

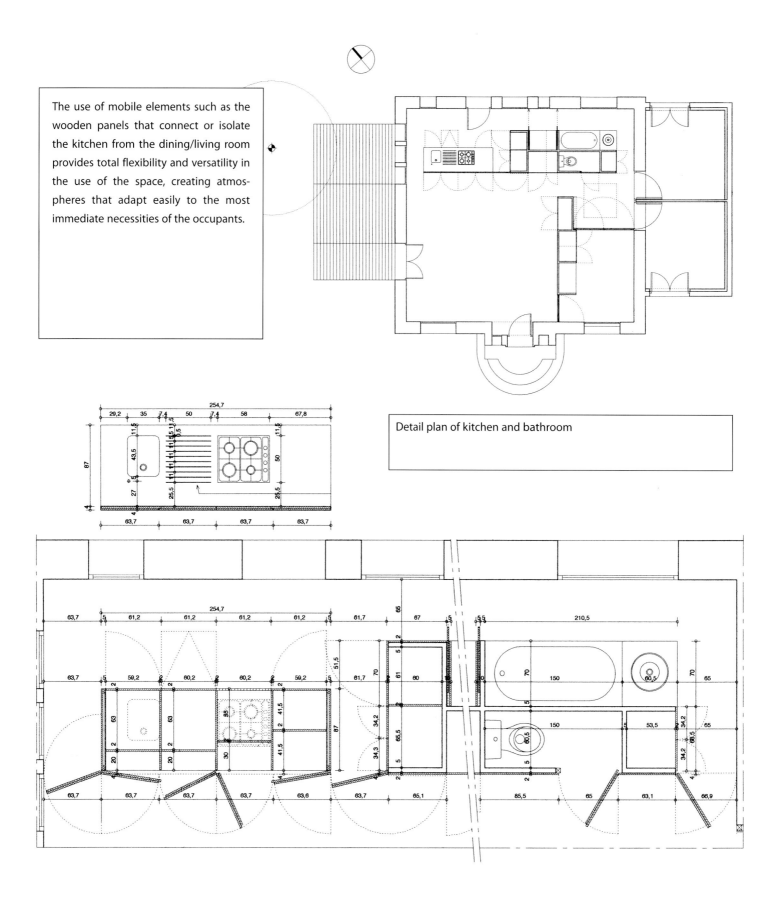

The use of mobile elements such as the wooden panels that connect or isolate the kitchen from the dining/living room provides total flexibility and versatility in the use of the space, creating atmospheres that adapt easily to the most immediate necessities of the occupants.

Detail plan of kitchen and bathroom

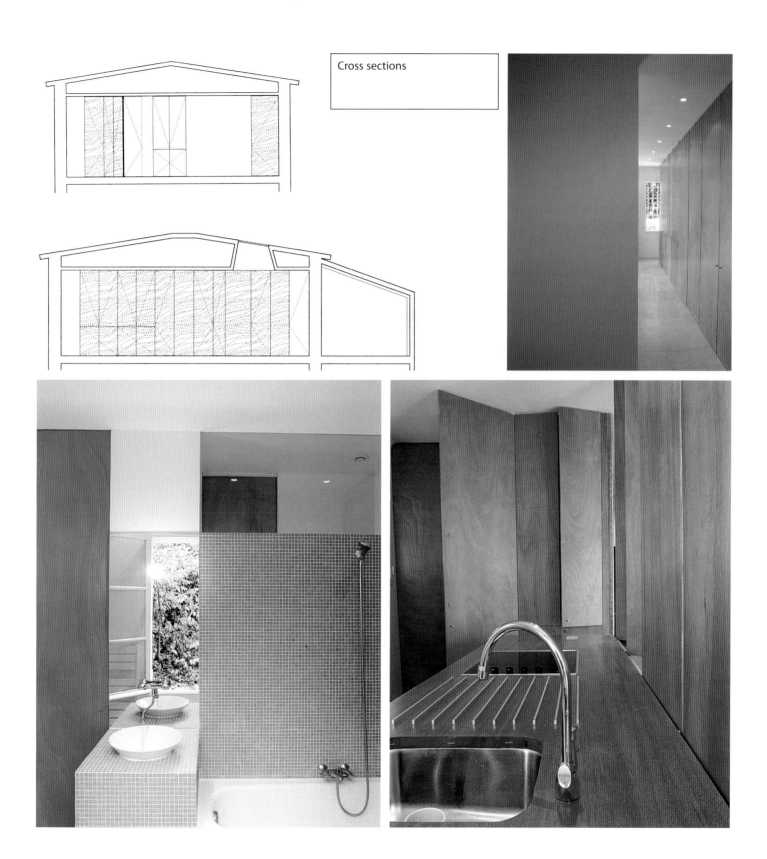

Cross sections

Penthouse T.O.

Vienna, Austria

Pool is Evelyn Rudnicki, Christoph Lammerhuber, Axel Linemayr and Florian Wallnöfer. They started cooperating in 1989 in what, together with others, was to become the BKK-2 team of architects, from 1993 to 1998. In 1998 they founded Pool Architektur ZT GmbH.

An essential feature of the Pool approach to design lies in the constant search for additional functional and emotional dimensions and in mixing them together and with the original scope of work, in order to charge space, a building or a city with energy and potential otherwise unsuspected. The enterprise contemplates projects of a public and/or a private nature. Bel-m, their entry for the Stadt 2000 town-planning competition for a Vienna district, was awarded the second prize in 1998. In 1999, penthouse was their solution to installing a whole apartment in 194 sqft (18 m²). The home designed for a single family in 2000 was awarded the Austrian Architect's Association Prize, and in 2002 they were given the State of Burgenland Architecture Prize for another private home, House S32.

Penthouse is the miniature apartment built in Vienna for Johannes Rudnicki in 1999, for a cost of 12,000 EUR including furniture. After about 5 months' planning, construction was carried out in little over a month.

194 sqft (18 m²) was the available space at one end of the roof of an industrial building that had previously carried a water tank. For structural reasons no further building load could be added to the rest of the existing roof. The only additional structures are the outdoor volumes into which most of the furniture can be pushed away when not in use: the bed, the table and the cupboard can slip in or out of the wall. The front of the room opens onto the roof terrace and enjoys an unimpeded perspective of the city. The kitchen unit is a sculptural steel console hung on the sloping wall over the staircase. The refrigerator has been hung from the ceiling. Opposite a fine old leather armchair, the TV set is housed on a swiveling platform, enabling it to be turned around to face the other side of the wall, the toilet. Formal finesse, an unconventional sense of fun and the visually ample environment have contributed to avoid any suspicion of claustrophobia.

In the words of the architects, "So small happiness can be".

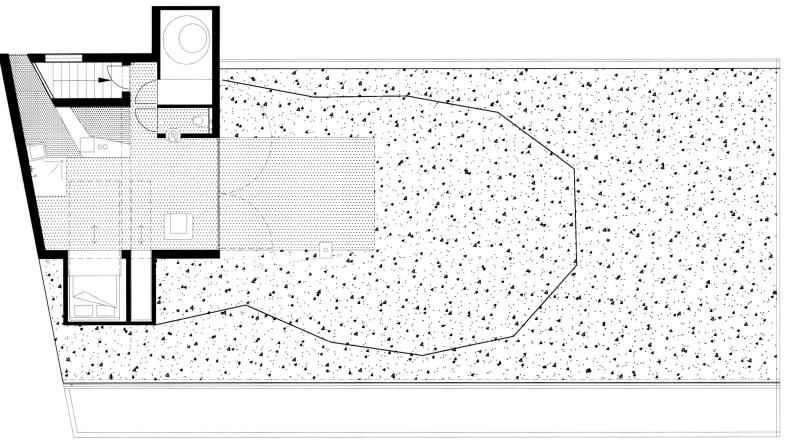

The front of the room opens onto the roof terrace end enjoys an unimpeded perspective of the city. The kitchen unit is a sculptural steel console hung on the sloping wall over the staircase. The refrigerator has been hung from the ceiling. Opposite a fine old leather armchair, the TV set is housed on a swiveling platform, enabling it to be turned around to face the other side of the wall, the toilet.

Home/Office for a Graphic Designer

New York, USA

The goal in this project was to create an interior which functioned as both home and office for a graphic designer within a modest 600 sqft (55 m^2) one bedroom apartment in Manhattan's West Village.

The challenge was to achieve this within a space which was too small to allot one room for an office without sacrificing the living/ dining room or the bedroom.

The solution was to remove the interior dividing wall and replace it with a structure that would allow the client to literally transform the living area into an office, and back again, on a daily basis.

The 13' long by 8' high freestanding structure divides the living room from the bedroom while allowing passage on both sides.

In the "home" position, the structure takes the form of a box, solid on all sides except for a deep, angled opening which offers selected views. A low, cushioned bench, both sofa and guest bed, cantilevers from the structure.

In the "work" position, the structure opens to transform the living room into an office. As the large bi-folding panels open, the cantilevered sofa automatically glides away and is concealed from view, and the two complete workstations are exposed.

When the workday is over and the large doors are closed, the sofa automatically returns to its position in the living room, and everything associated with work, including computers, printers and cables, is completely concealed.

The dining table also moves in a controlled path, gliding within a channel in the top of the wall cabinet. The table glides out into the room for dining, when the office is closed, and it glides back against the wall and doubles as a workspace when the office is open.

On the bedroom side, the structure acts as a tall wooden headboard for the bed, while housing recessed night-tables which fold down on either side.

www.rogerhirsch.com

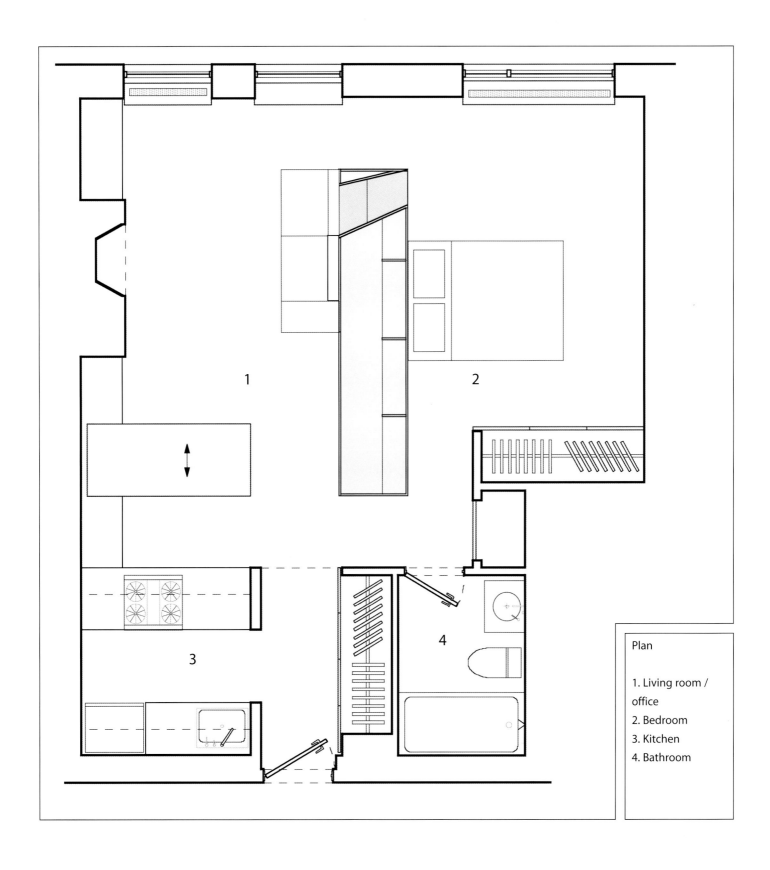

Plan

1. Living room /
office
2. Bedroom
3. Kitchen
4. Bathroom

In the "work" position, the structure opens to transform the living room into an office. As the large bi-folding panels open, the cantilevered sofa automatically glides away and is concealed from view, and the two complete workstations are exposed. When the workday is over and the large doors are being closed, the sofa automatically returns to its position in the living room, and everything associated with work, including computers, printers and cables are completely concealed.

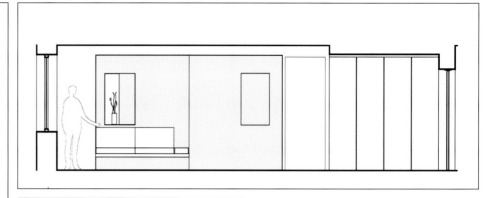

Elevation - Office unit closed

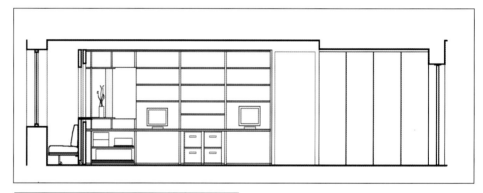

Elevation - Office unit open

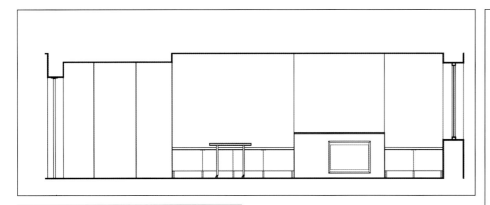

Elevation - built-in cabin with sliding table

The 13' long by 8' high freestanding structure divides the living room from the bedroom while allowing passage on both sides. The dining table also moves in a controlled path, gliding within a channel in the top of the wall cabinet. The table glides out into the room for dining, when the office is closed, and it glides back against the wall and doubles as a workspace when the office is open. On the bedroom side, the structure acts as a tall wooden headboard for the bed, while housing recessed night-tables which fold down on either side.

Juan Pablo Molestina/Gruppe MDK+Aysin Ipekci

Photographs:
Contributed by Gruppe MDK

Archilab LivingRoom

Orléans, France

The Archilab exhibition is about architecture and dwelling. The idea is to present three architectural projects which deal with the theme of dwelling, but to do so in such a way that the viewer is held in a familiar, living-room-like atmosphere while being shown the projects.

The main exhibit piece, a moveable red exhibition box, opens into a miniaturized living-room: a sofa unfolds from the flat cover, complete with a shag carpet, a foot-light and an aquarium, and reveals a typical living room cupboard with shelves and drawers where architectural models are found.

At the center of the back-lit cupboard, in a recessed niche, there is a television set which is always on. One should have the impression that this TV set is showing normal family television, and that there is the possibility, through the pressing of the video button, of watching a home made video movie.

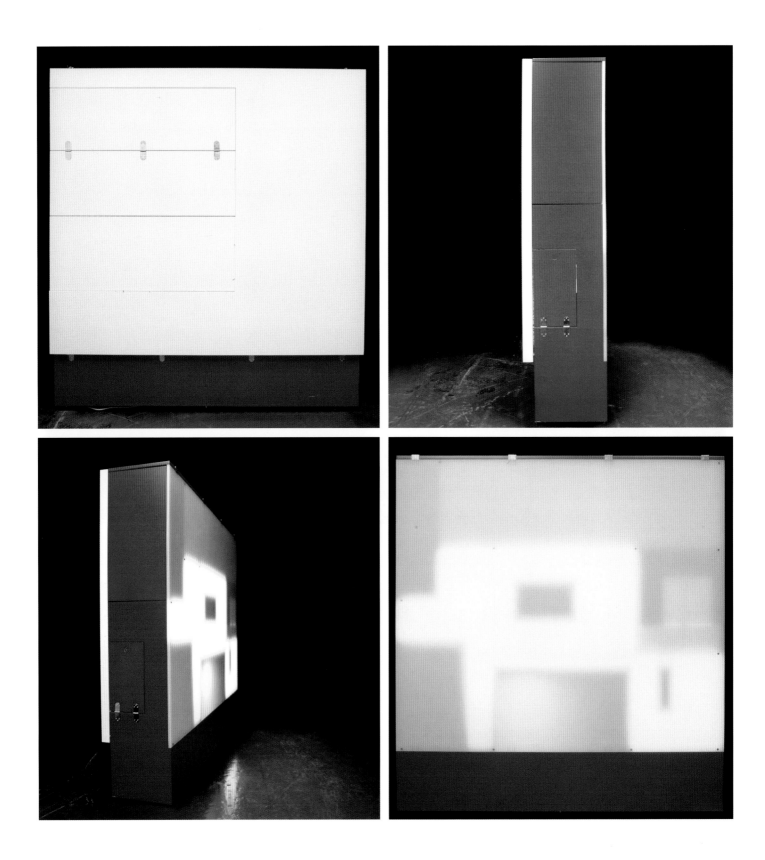

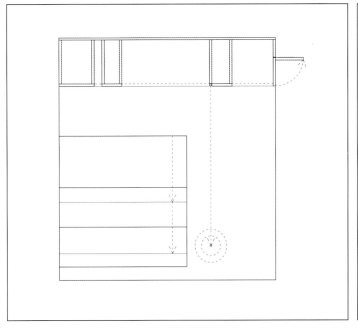

Plan 1

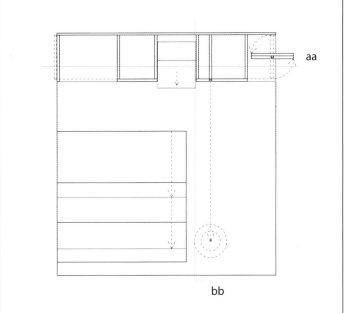

aa

bb

Plan 2

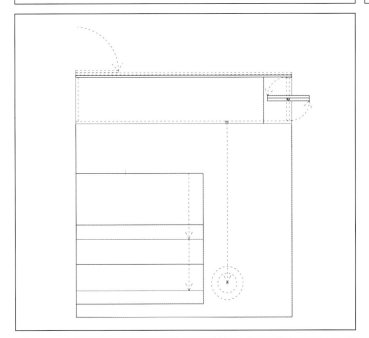

Plan 3

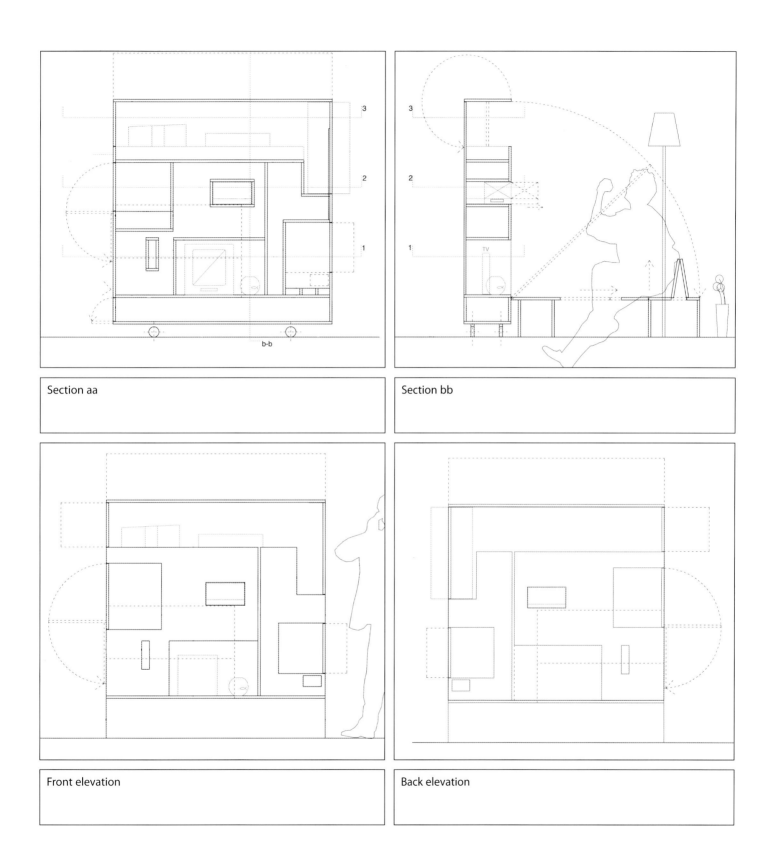

Section aa

Section bb

Front elevation

Back elevation

Suitcase house

Badaling Shuiguan, Beijing,
People's Republic of China

In 2000, SOHO China Ltd. invited 12 young architects from South Korea, Japan, Taiwan, Singapore, Thailand, Mainland China and Hong Kong, to design 11 houses and a clubhouse in the valley at the foot of the Great Wall.

Rethinking the proverbial image of a house, Suitcase House Hotel questions the nature of intimacy, privacy, spontaneity and flexibility, in pursuit of infinite adaptable scenarios, unfolding the mechanics of domestic (p)leisure.

The 2696.356 sqft (250.5 m²) building, completed in October 2001 at the head of the Nangou Valley, is oriented to maximize views of the Great Wall and solar exposure in the temperate continental climate.

The base of the building's three strata is a concrete plinth, which contains the pantry, a servant's room, the boiler room and the sauna.

The middle layer cantilevers outward from the concrete plinth that anchors the steel structure above. Everything is clad in the same timber, blurring boundaries between in and out, building and furniture. This level is for habitation, activity and flow. The layout is non-hierarchical; movable items of the shell adapt to the activity, number of occupants, or preferences regarding privacy. The open volume turns into a sequence of rooms, each singularized by a specific role. Concealed under a landscape of pneumatically assisted floor panels, several function-specific compartments may be "unfolded". Only what is in use is present at any one time. Besides the basic bedroom, bathroom, kitchen and storage, there is a meditation chamber (with glazed floor looking down the valley), music chamber, library, study, lounge, and a fully equipped sauna. If guests arrive in the evening, the entire space, 144 x161/2ft (44 x 5 m), can turn into a single lounge. If the party goes on late, seven guest rooms can be unfolded, accommodating up to 14 people.

The exterior is an envelope of full height double-glazed folding doors; the inner layer is a series of screens. The façade pattern is rooted in its user-oriented logic. The various entrances hold equal status and their use decides the distribution.

A pull-down ladder leads to the roof, the top stratum, with a 360º view.

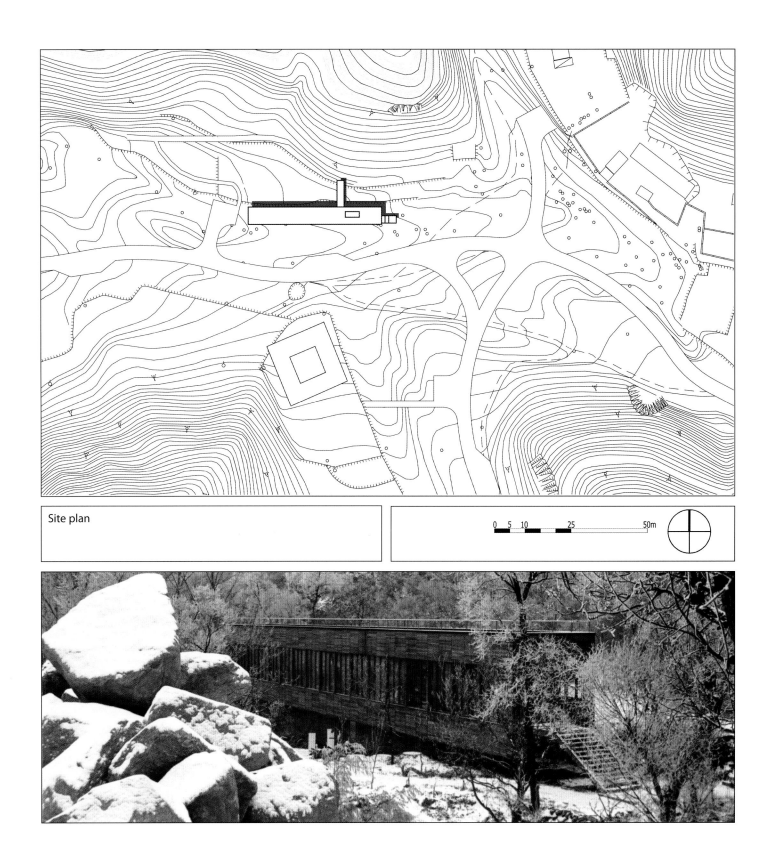

Site plan

0 5 10 25 50m

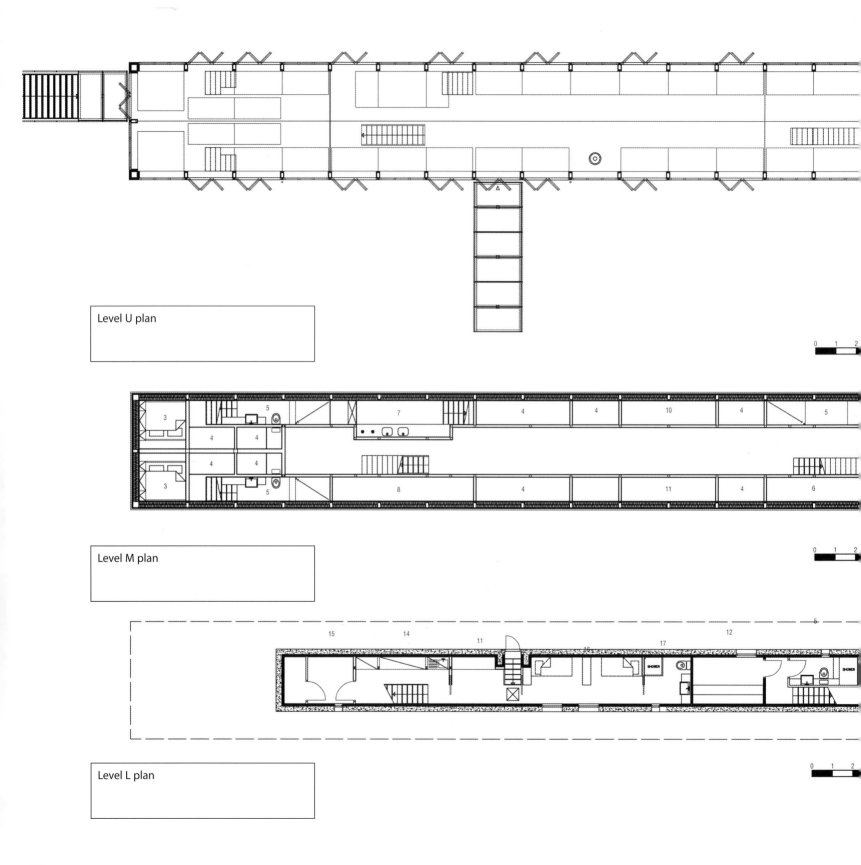

Level U plan

Level M plan

Level L plan

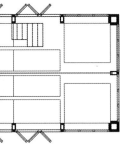

5   10m

1. Living
2. Dining
3. Bedroom
4. Storage
5. Bathing
6. Study
7. Kitchen
8. Cloak room
9. Meditation
10. Audio/visual
11. Library
12. Sauna
13. Laundry
14. Pantry
15. Boiler room
16. Butler's bedroom
17. Butler's bathroom

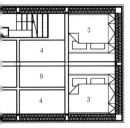

5   10m

5   10m

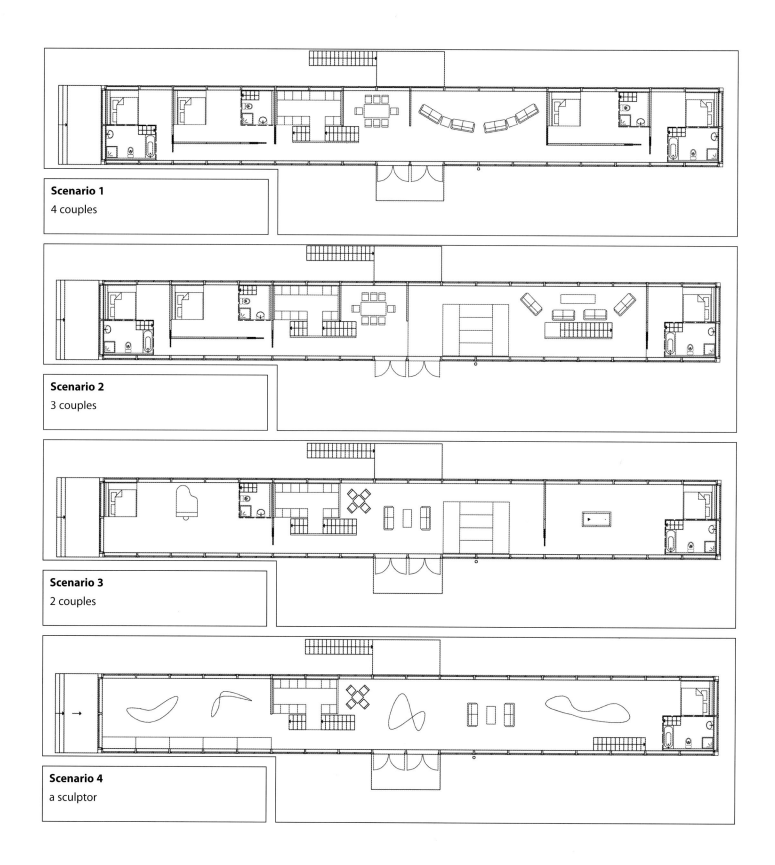

Scenario 1
4 couples

Scenario 2
3 couples

Scenario 3
2 couples

Scenario 4
a sculptor

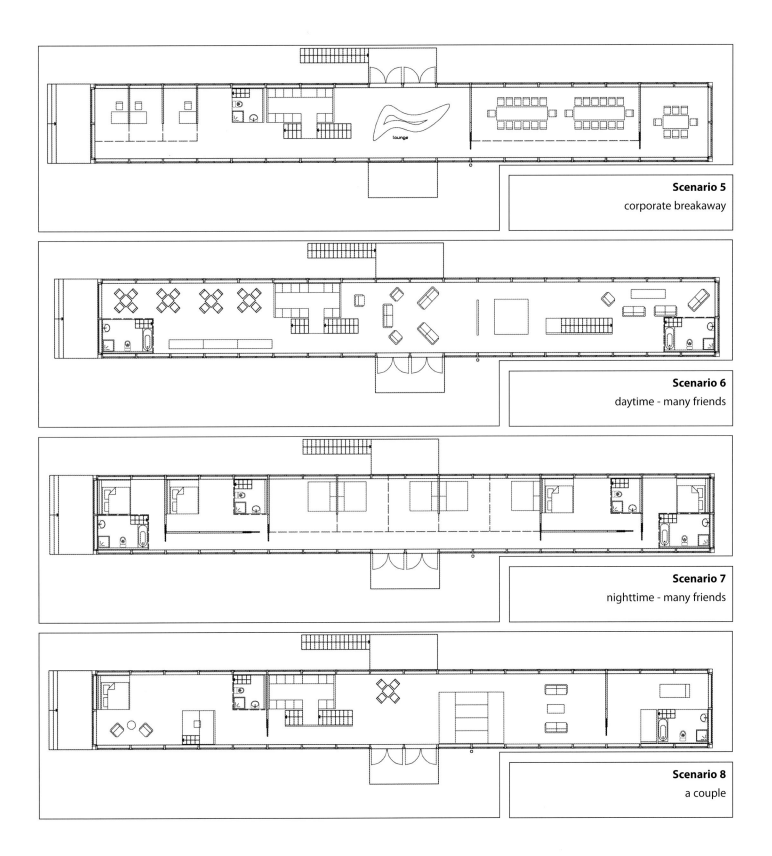

Scenario 5

corporate breakaway

Scenario 6

daytime - many friends

Scenario 7

nighttime - many friends

Scenario 8

a couple

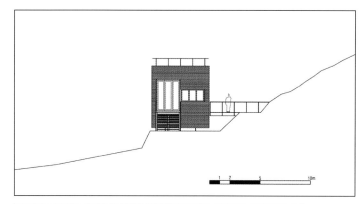

East elevation

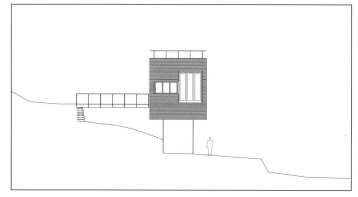

West elevation

South elevation

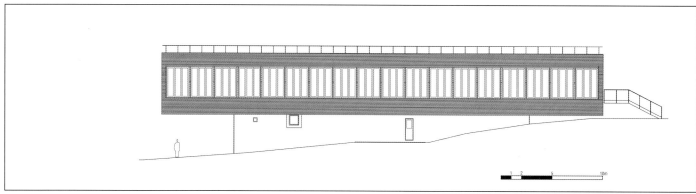

Pneumatically assisted floor panel	1. Location of latch	
	2. Location of dead-bolt	5. Recessed hinge
	3. Gas spring	6. Metal bracket
	4. Location of hook and eye to hold panel in position	7. Under panel support

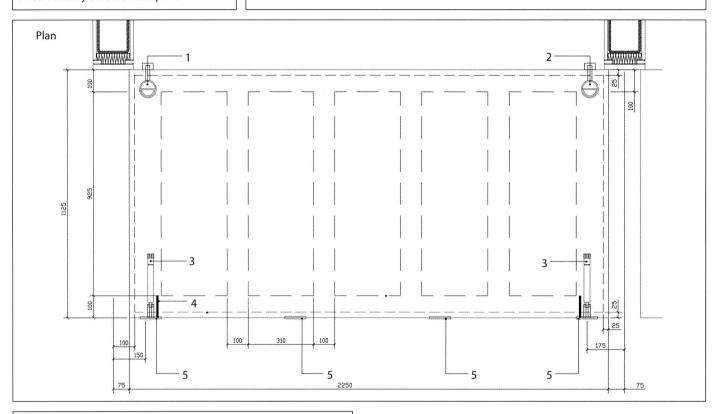

Plan

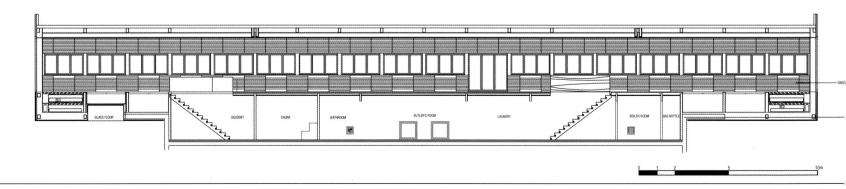

Interior elevations

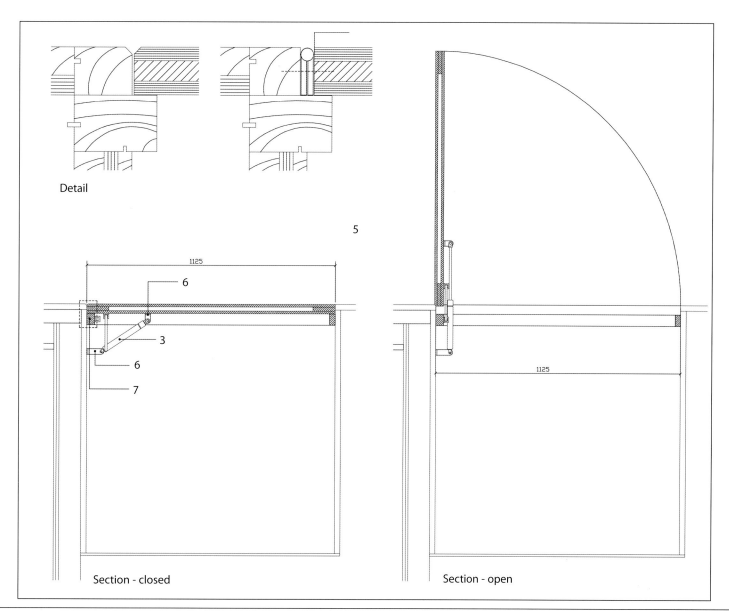

Detail

5

1125

6

6

3

7

Section - closed

1125

Section - open

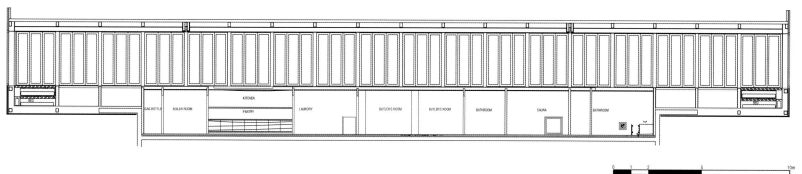

GAS BOTTLE BOILER ROOM KITCHEN LAUNDRY BUTLER'S ROOM BUTLER'S ROOM BATHROOM SAUNA BATHROOM

PANTRY

0 1 2 5 10m

Bathroom

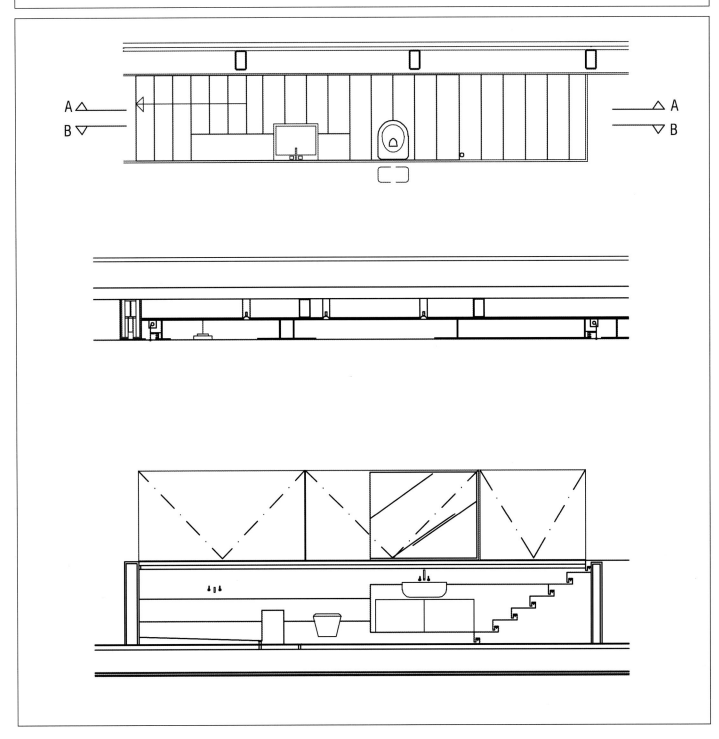

A △   △ A
B ▽   ▽ B

Kitchen

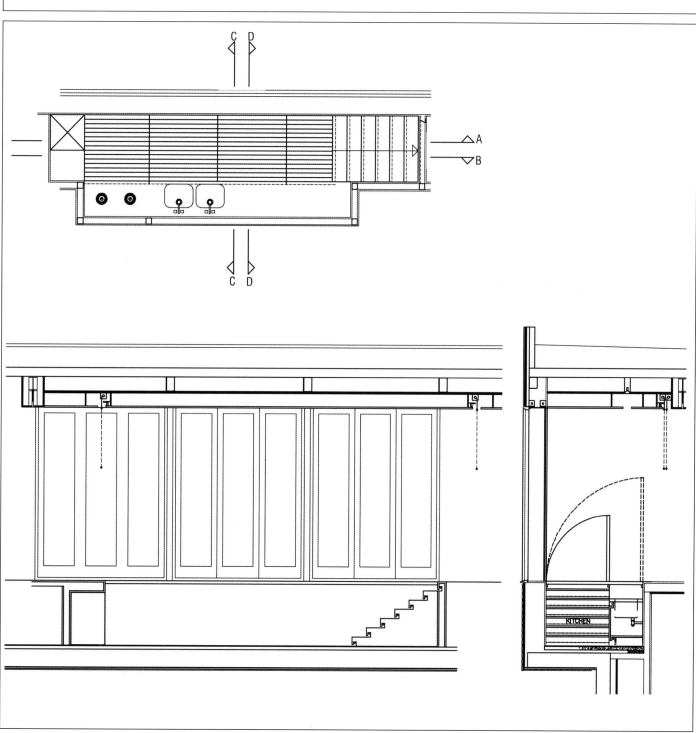

KITCHEN

SPLTTERWERK

Photographs:
Paull Ott,
Splitterwerk

Black Treefrog

Bad Waltersdorf, Austria

For over 20 years SPLITTERWERK has researched the "dematerialization" of architecture, questioning traditional relationships between form, function and construction, addressing the idea of flowing spatial continuums in the 21st century with their "Multiincident Shell", a metamorphic, media informed living experience. The walls allow functions to be added as desired. Research into experimental coatings and reliefs, computer-generated ornaments, electronically controlled interactive projections or self-illuminating surfaces, has led SPLITTERWERK to restate the question of structure and ornament leading to a new figurative architecture. The ornament is the building is the medium is the message.

The starting point at Bad Waltersdorf was a nondescript two-wing building with an added garage for the fire brigade.

This was dressed with a wooden trellis dyed black that vines are already growing on, to integrate the façades. The 10 apartments or dwelling units inside are independent of the outer walls. Surrounded by a coloured plywood skin, the space in between the inner and outer wall houses unfoldable functional spaces. In the center is a functionless space which each specific living function can occupy concurrently or successively.

Blue Shell and Ivory Fresh Shell in the Black Treefrog are Multiincident Shells defined by the requirments of dwelling. The Ivory Shell is only 345 sqft (32 m^2); of which 194 sqft (18 m^2) are the "functionally neutral zone". The other 151sqft (14 m^2) contain all the specific domestic functions, each of which can be individually unfolded and opened into the neutral zone. Hall, kitchen, dining space or living room can be brought out, each of which totals 1940 sqft (18 m^2). The sum of the different functional floor areas is equivalent to an apartment of 194 sqft (180 m^2) . These multiincident dwelling units can be connected to each other. The new interior envelope is conceived as a continuously active media surface. Projections, enlarged picture screens or TV can make the spatial divisions into virtual events.

101

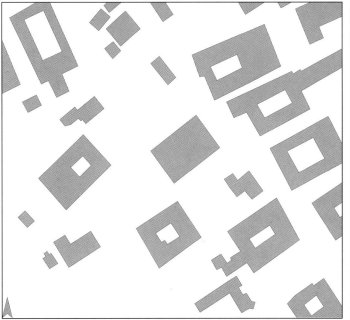

Open elevations
East, North, West

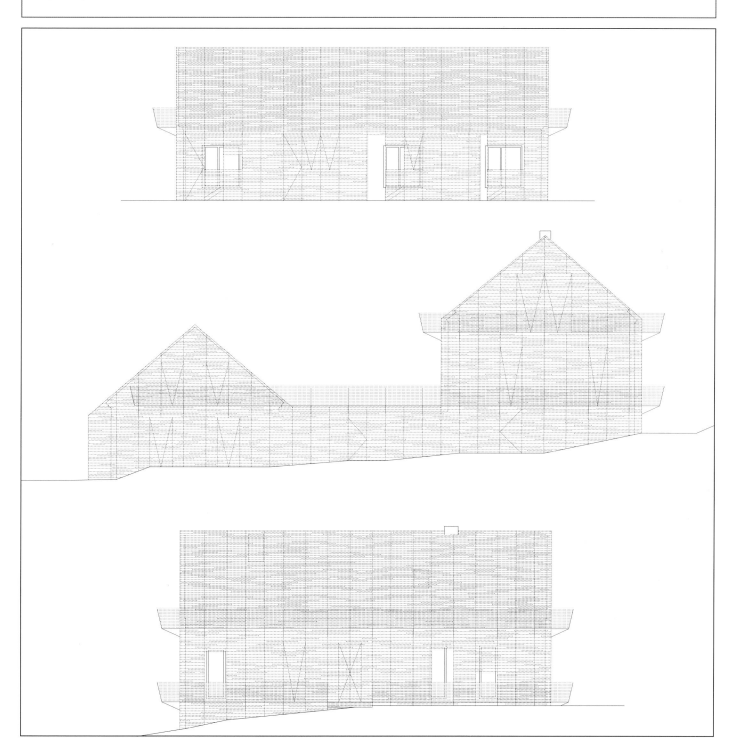

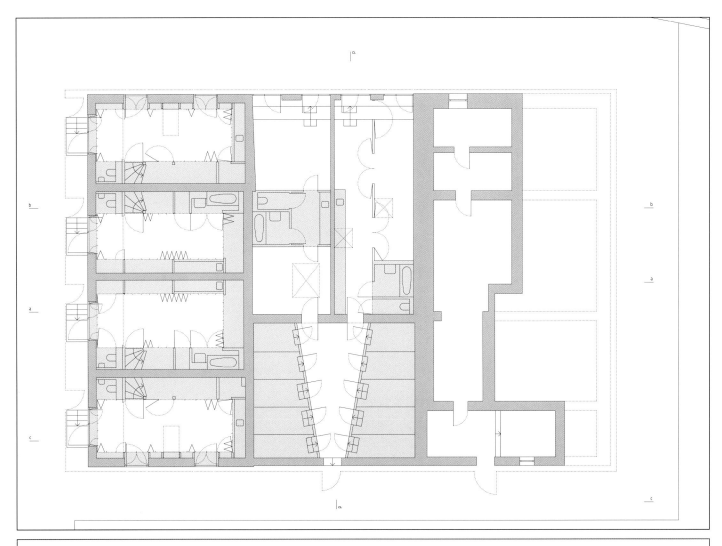

Ground floor

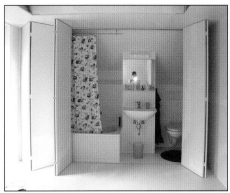

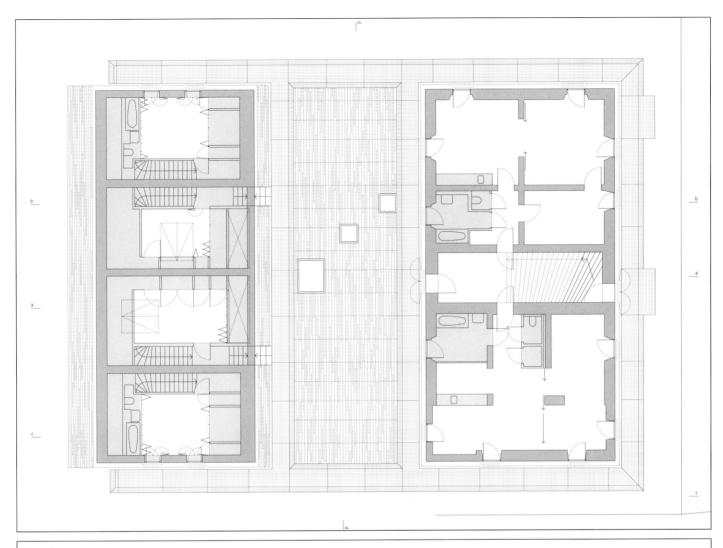

First floor

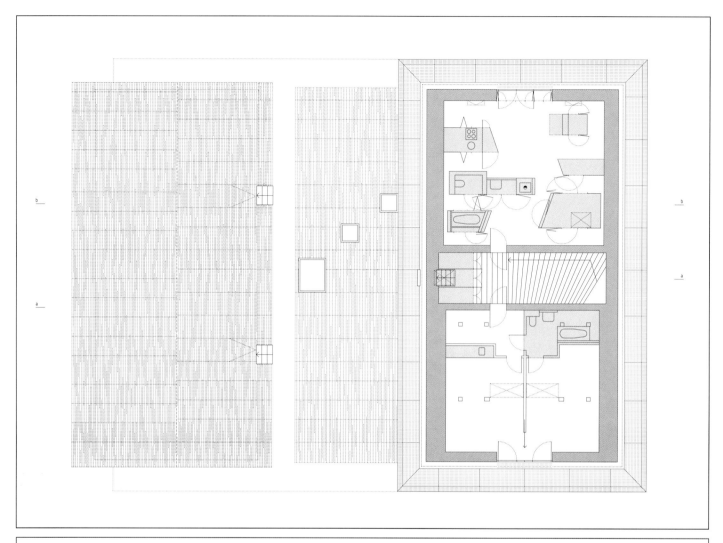

Second floor

Section AA

Section BB

blue shell

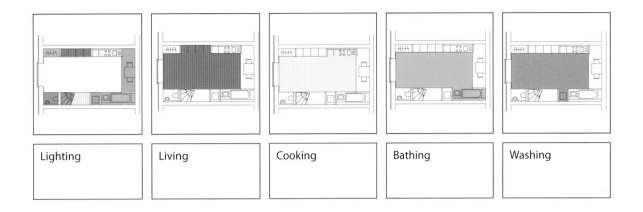

| Lighting | Living | Cooking | Bathing | Washing |

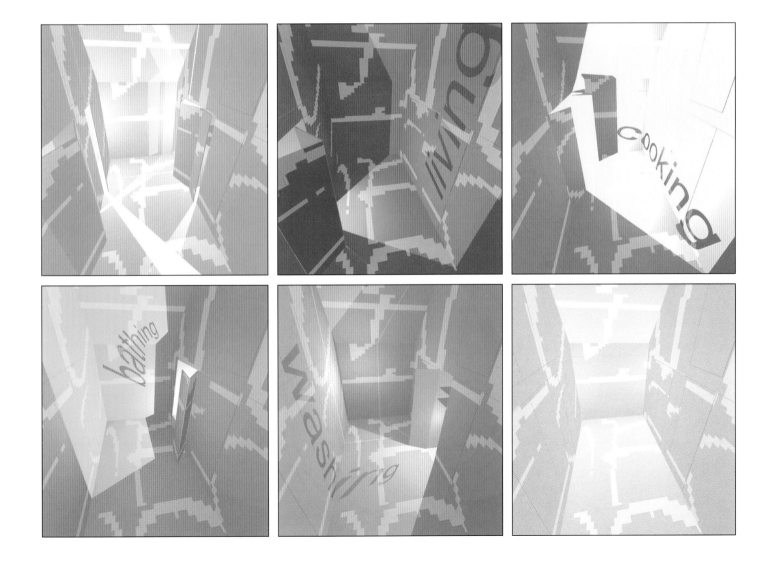

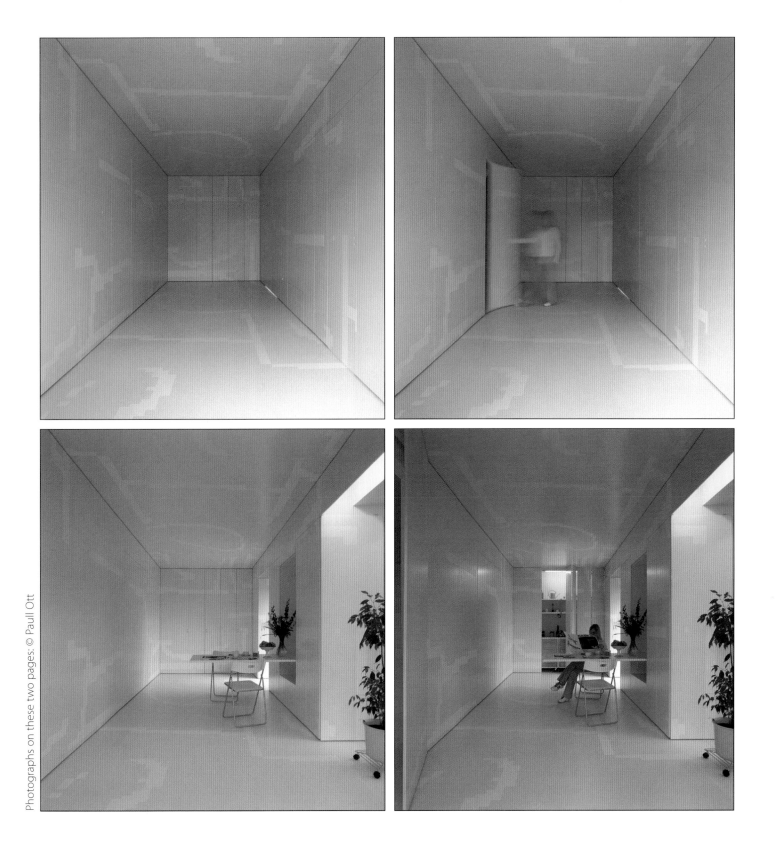

Sturm und Wartzech

Photographs:
contributed by the architects

Kubus

Dipperz, Germany

The foreseeable ultimate form of the project would involve the production of the various functional units of a house accommodated in spatially autonomous cubes; in moving from room to room one necessarily passes into the open air, stepping onto the ground out-doors, which is an essential part of the idea of living in the midst of nature. The first functional unit to have been carried out so far is the living cube. It is enclosed on three sides by timber-panel walls with a high degree of thermal insulation. This cell is supplied with electricity by photovoltaic panels and is virtually self-sufficient in terms of energy needs. The fourth wall consists of triple low-E glazing with a xenon filling. This ensures considerable energy gains, even in the wintertime. It also helps to create a sense of spaciousness despite the limited room size, affording panoramic views of the world outside. Visual privacy and protection against glare are provided by a screen that rises from the base. In the closed wall and soffit areas, a top-hung window and a roof light frame further views of the fields and the sky. Stools and a tabletop fold out from the wall under the side-window and other furnishings can be drawn or pivoted out from the other wall, to transform the geometry of the abstract meditative space into a functional realm for living, working and sleeping. The cube is raised from the ground on a rotating central pivot supported by economic ball bearings of the type used in conventional vehicle construction. Besides creating a more dynamic discourse with the surroundings, this enables the inhabitants to control the view out of the structure and heat gains from the sun through the large glazed façade by manually turning the cube to face the appropriate direction.

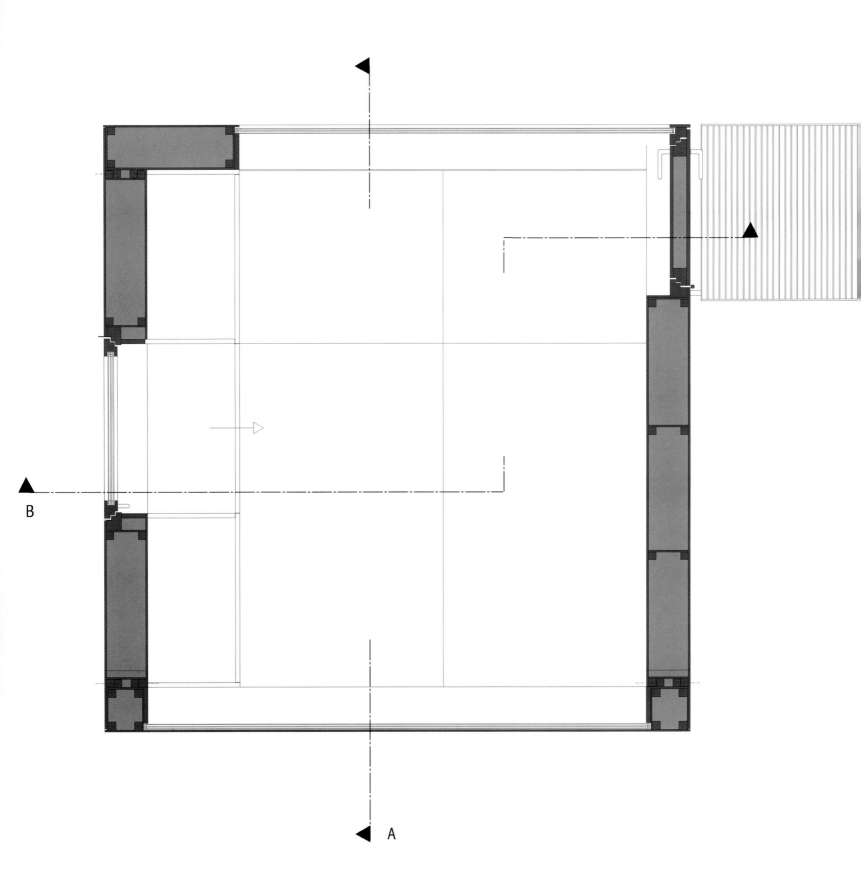

B

A

A

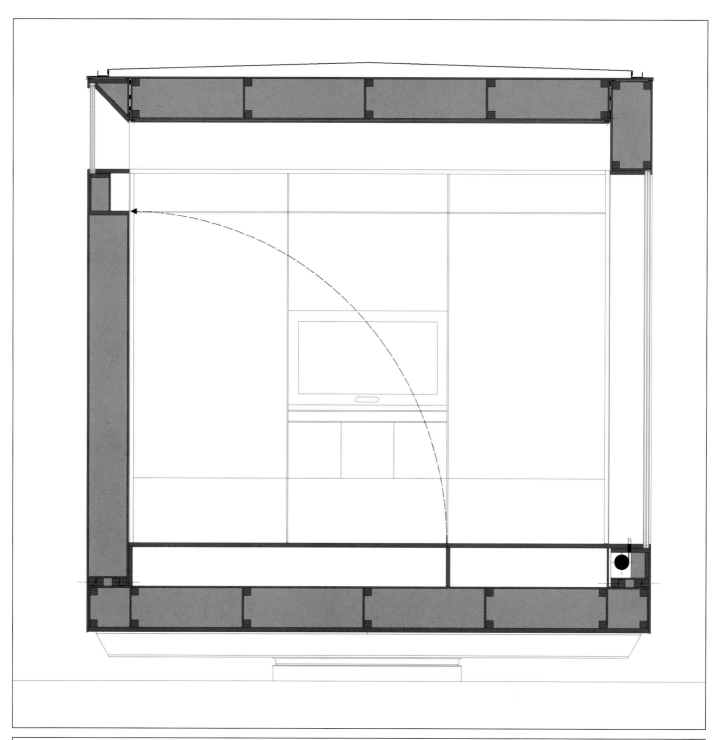

Section AA

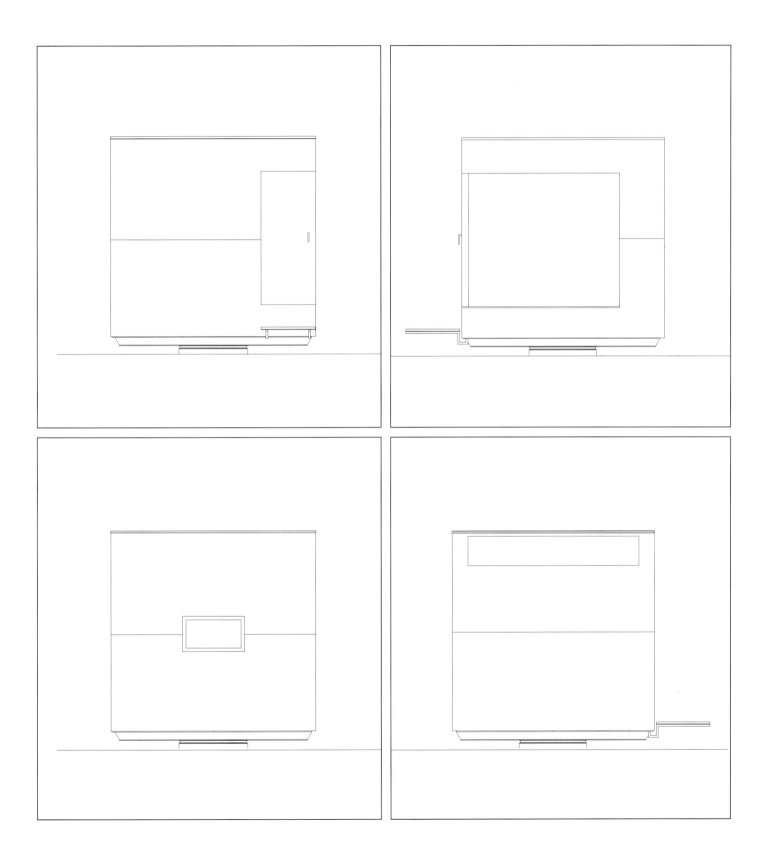

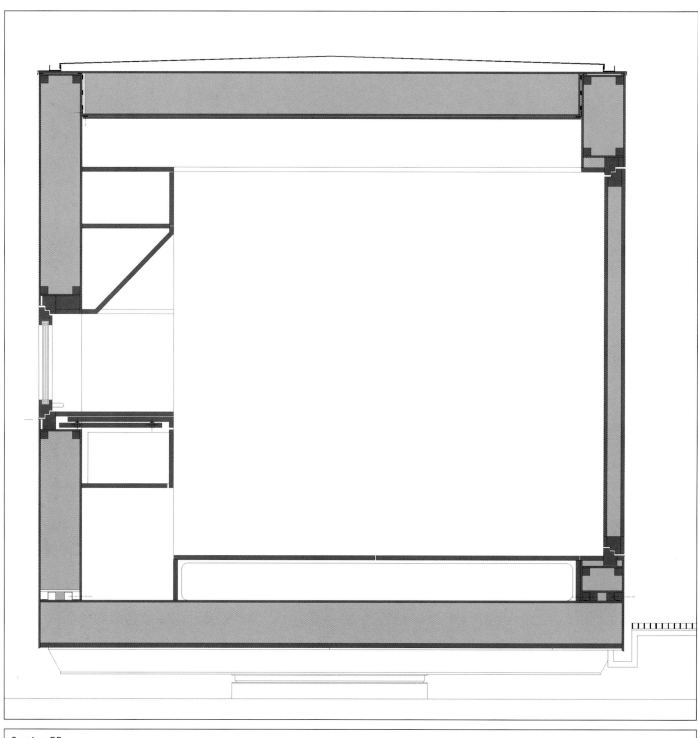

Section BB

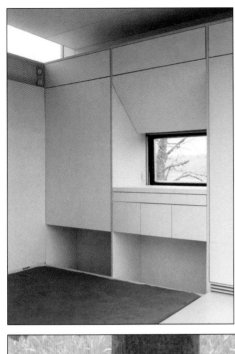

Eva Prats y Ricardo Flores

Photographs:
Eugeni Pons

A house in a suitcase

Barcelona, Spain

The concept was carried out in an attic of Barcelona's Ensanche district. The rectangular space is 3 m wide and high, by 9 m long. There is a small space on the side with the sanitary installation, which doesn't regard the present considerations. The only opening outdoors is the skylight that runs down the full length of the room. It is a temporary dwelling, used by people who travel a lot with little luggage. The apartment only contains the zenithal light that floods it and two large closed volumes. These pieces of furniture have been designed like the trunks of the great travelers, the content dictating the container (let's remember the compact traveling wardrobes and writing desks invented by Louis Vuitton, which opened up to become pieces of furniture with all a person's needs).

The reduced space doesn't permit objects to accumulate and one of the guidelines of the design was to prevent dust from gathering during the periods when it is empty.

The project researches the minimum occupation our activities require; the trunks open their various facets revealing unguessed uses which divide the space into fragments at a human scale, for precise chores. The free space varies in form and function throughout the day.

The larger body contains the largest object, the bed, and also the smallest: a sliding shelf to place jewelry or pills. The doors of the dormitory trunk act as a screen to conceal dressing or undressing. It also has a luggage rack, a mirror and two bedside tables with reading lamps and a drawer for the bedclothes. The bed slides away under the hall landing and the bed head can double as a sofa back.

Out of the kitchen trunk slide shelves and tables. An upper shelf hides the kitchen from the entrance hall. A breakfast table slides out next to the china cupboard and the larder.

Before leaving everything is hidden again.

Until the next visit the door closes on a room full of light and two giant traveling trunks.

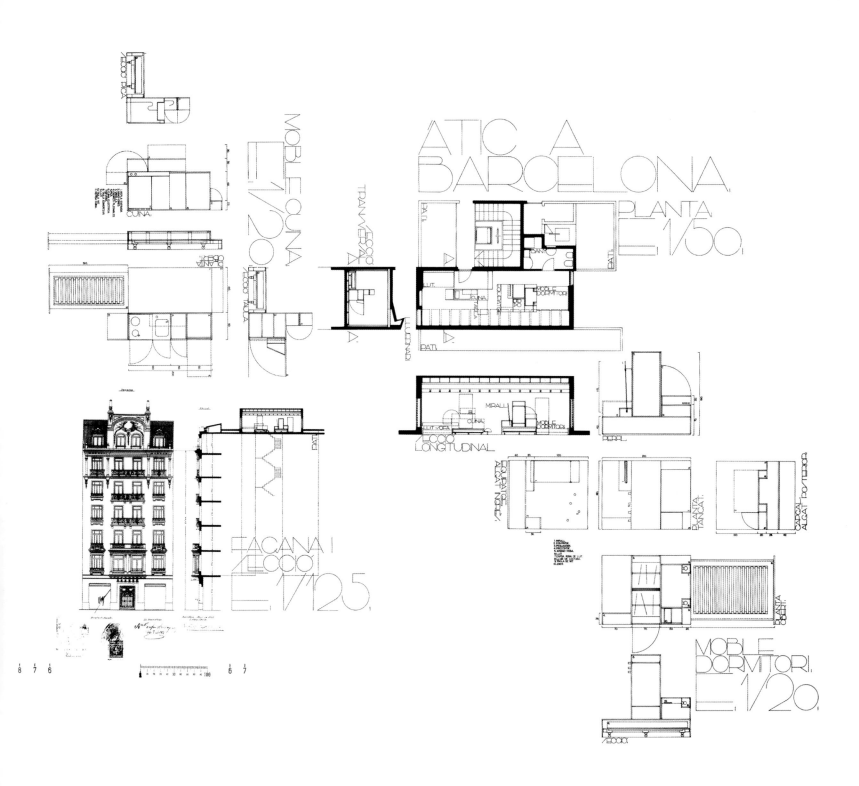

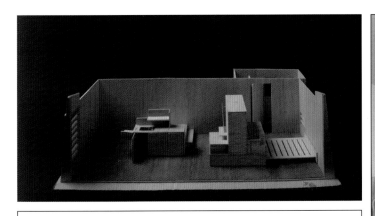

Dimensions of the space: 9x3x3.
Dimensions of the dormitory trunk: 2,10m x 1,60m x 1,90m high.
Dimensions of the kitchen trunk: 2,00m x 1,65m x 1,20m high.

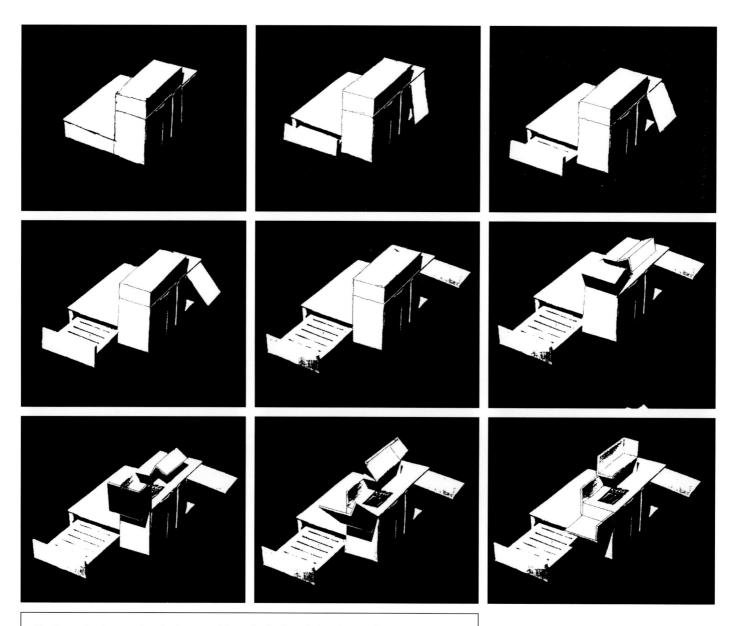

The larger body contains the largest object, the bed, and also the smallest: a sliding shelf to place jewelry or pills. The doors of the dormitory trunk act as a screen to conceal dressing or undressing. It also has a luggage rack, a mirror and two beside tables with reading lamps and a drawer for the bedclothes. The bed slides away under the hall landing and the bed head can double as a sofa back.

Before leaving everything is hidden again.
Until the next visit the door closes on a room full of light and two giant traveling trunks.

Mies.update
Study for contemporary flexible dwelling

Stuttgart , Germany

Taking up Mies van der Rohe's ideas of the "greatest possible liberty in the manner of use" or the "flowing space" the project interprets the floorplans of its apartment building, "Weissenhof 14-20", within the context of contemporary life-styles, techniques and materials.

The combination of typified mobile items of furniture with space containing pneumatic walls provides different options regarding the organization, the distribution and the atmosphere of a space. While the hard wall shell takes up technical infrastructures, the extendable pneumatic volumes can be deformed freely in a three-dimensional sense, fulfilling the functions of both wall and furniture, simultaneously or alternatively.

These volumes can be individualized or adapted by means of new coatings with heat, light or electrical conductivity.

Opaque or translucent treatments create sight- and sound-proof divisions, while a transparent version separates different functions by creating almost invisible barriers. The hollow nature of these barriers enables them to carry heated or cooled air, or light.

Breaking up the conventional space categories and hierarchies, such a "living" structure can be constantly adapted to the users' short and long-term needs.

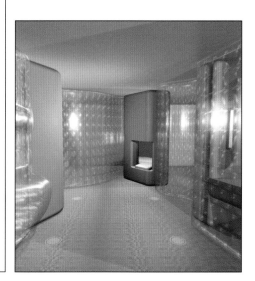

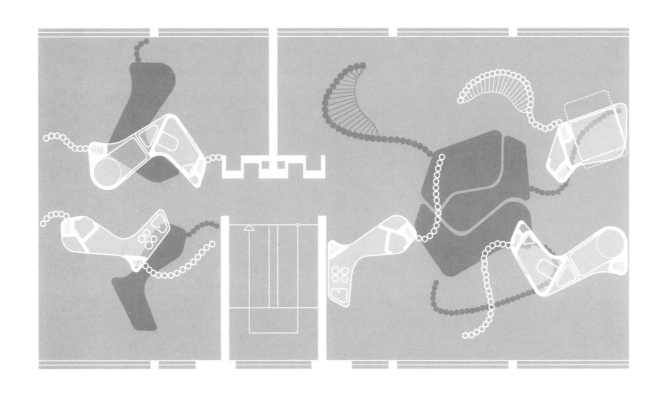

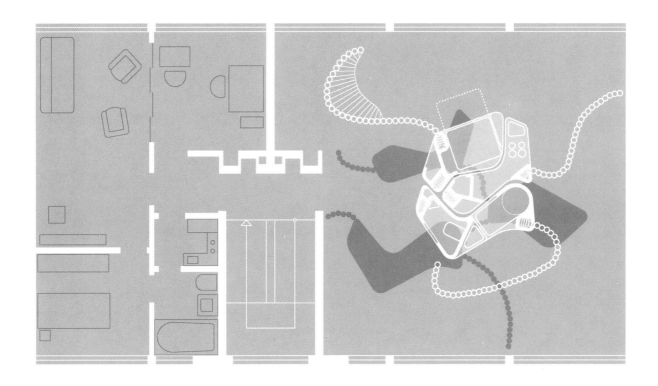

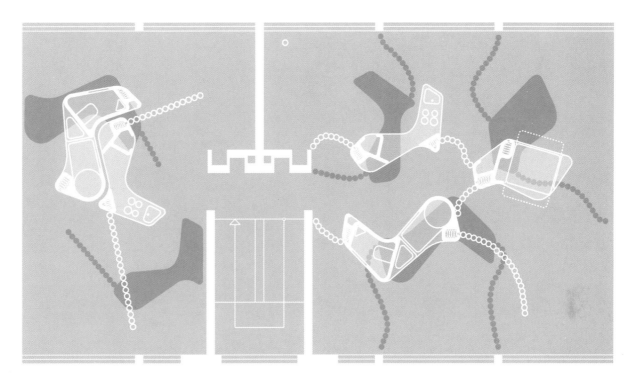

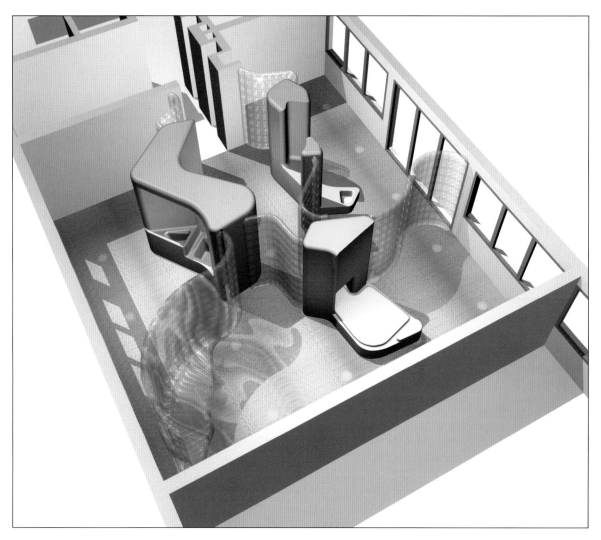

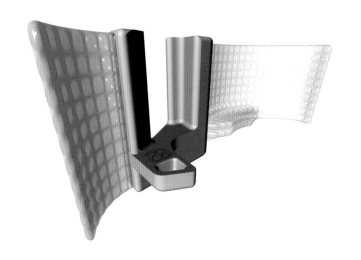

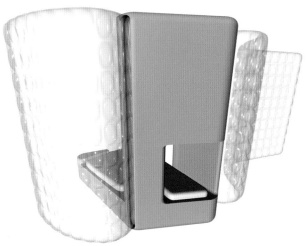

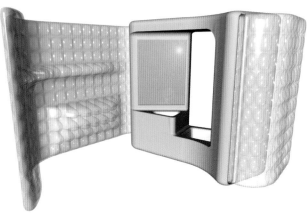

Blauraum Architekten

Photographs:
Jörg Hempel,
Blauraum Architekten

Salon Blauraum

Hamburg, Germany

Contemporary architecture and its concerns seem very foreign in Hamburg, a city of traders where the solid language of quick return is readily understood and respected. Corporate architectural firms control most of the market, and the numerous independent architects, less economically heavy-handed, are invited to sell their souls for the scraps.

When Rüdiger Ebel, Volker Halbach, Maurice Paulussen and Carsten Venus decided to start their practice here, they became aware it wasn't enough to find office space and go for it. One would have to create office space in a broader sense: a space of discourse and discussion from which a genuine architectural scene could emerge. So the four young architects started their office, Blauraum Architekten, and at the same time Salon Blauraum, as a forum specialized in design. More than a Café or a Gallery, the object is to maintain communication.

Both premises have separate entrances. Of the three street windows, the Salon has two. The first impression is of a closed cube, which then reveals its capacity to unfold by means of a series of hinged screens. One section displays a snack bar inside it, with a concealed kitchen work surface and a beautiful expresso machine. Another sector swivels around a central pivot, opening the way to a long corridor leading to various office spaces (conference room, plotter space).

The walls are faced with cork, to which office documents and notes can be pinned, as well as exhibits from the Salon. Office staff and Salon visitors mingle in the corridor, producing a creatively-stimulating overlap of work and play. In fact everything in the office is movable and can make room for larger public events or lectures.

The Salon provides an uncramped yet appropriate scenario for Blauraum architects to meet their clients. The unconventional work context is underlined by atmospheric lighting and glowing Formica desktops, bright textile hangings and comfortable chairs, a contemporary living room.

In the Salon the vertical boxes not only serve as espresso tables but as gallery pedestals. Thus the white cube gallery cliché is drawn towards the cocktail lounge ambience, and the cork wall tempts the public to become part of the show.

Photographs on this page: © Blauraum Architekten

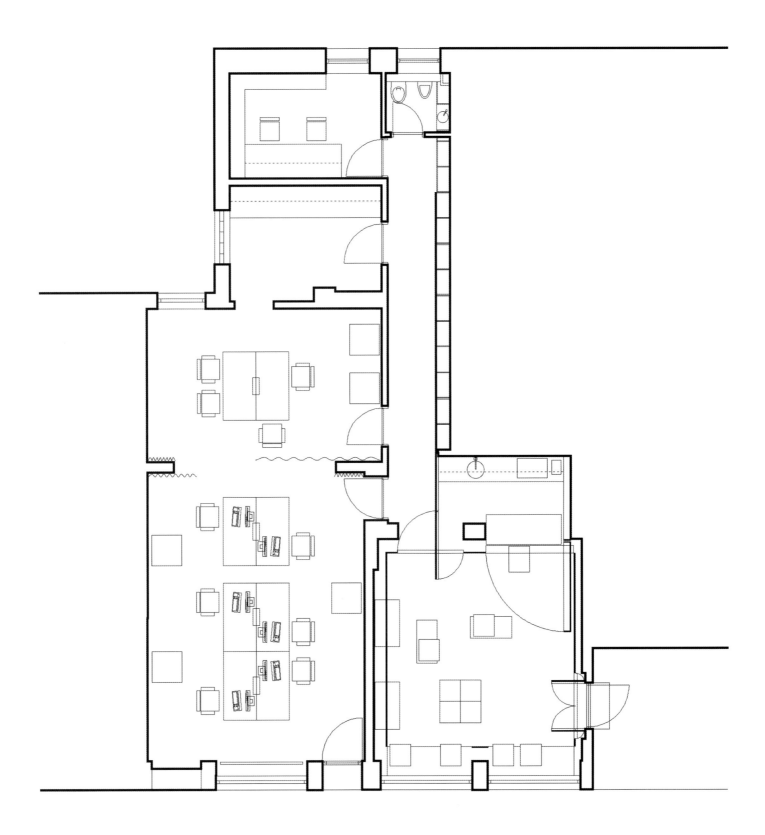

138

The four young architects started their office, Blauraum Architekten, and at the same time Salon Blauraum, as a forum specialized in design. To ensure a prominent profile they secured the premises on a busy street in the city center, a former shop with large display windows. One part of the shop took their offices. In the other a café with a design-oriented exhibition space was opened to attract the public and prompt conversation.

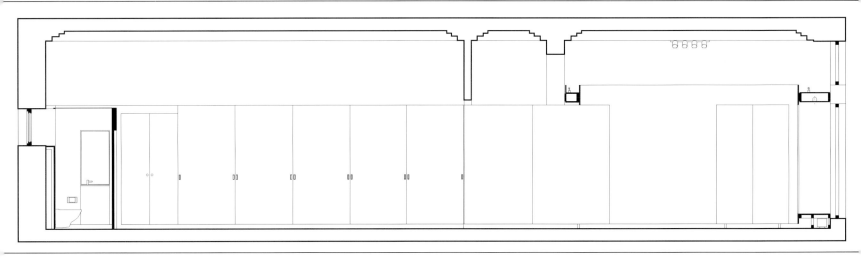

Section through corridor

The first impression is of a closed cube, which then reveals its capacity to unfold by means of a series of hinged screens. One section displays a snack bar inside it, with a concealed kitchen work surface and a beautiful espresso machine. Another sector swivels around a central pivot, opening the way to a long corridor leading to various office spaces (conference room, plotter space). The walls are faced with cork, to which office documents and notes can be pinned, as well as exhibits from the Salon.

Urs Hartmann, Markus Wetzel

Photographs:
Menga von Sprecher,
Urs Hartmann

Wildbrook

Zürich, Switzerland

Within the architectural context of a loft renovation, two artists built a bathroom and a kitchen as part of a 3-month art performance, blurring the line between art and domestic infrastructure.

The artists made the process of fabrication and installation into an on site art action. Until it concluded, the objects were tools, accessories, works of art and stage props all in one. Although their final role in the apartment defines them as sanitary appliances, their development has not concluded. This bathroom and kitchen can be turned around and pushed about. The two docking stations for connecting to the water and electrical system permit six different combinations and a constantly changing experience; the loft will inherit a dynamic quality from its temporary use as an art installation. The bare unfinished walls and floor add to the "work in progress" impression of artists' studios in the sixties, although this is not a derelict factory but an expensive urban space in a sophisticated district of Zurich. On a rolling wooden platform stand two amorphous fiberglass shapes that contain the bathroom. The two forms are connected. A large door leads inside, where a small hole allows one to slip through into the bath. The kitchen, also fiberglass, is formally less experimental. Ceiling slats and corrugated cardboard make up the body, which is stabilized with a layer of polyester. Instead of walls, the rolling kitchen has a metal curtain.

Everybody in building is aware of a growing demand for individualized solutions. The wildbrook project satisfies these requirements so far as to consider the clients changing future needs. The limitation of the artists' skill as craftsmen is raised to the status of an aesthetic credo. Everything works perfectly but the plumbing and lighting fixtures have a slapdash temporary look. The unfinished DIY atmosphere invites further self-done interventions and is a stand against predominant ultra-slick environments. The amateurish touch of the interiors rubs provocatively against the precious finish of the architectural shell. The whole process was recorded in the film "sweet Wildbrook".

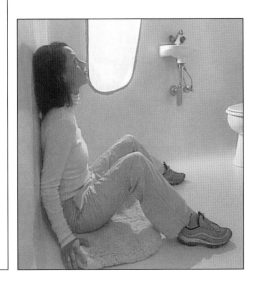

Stills from the film and photgraphs of the construction process

147

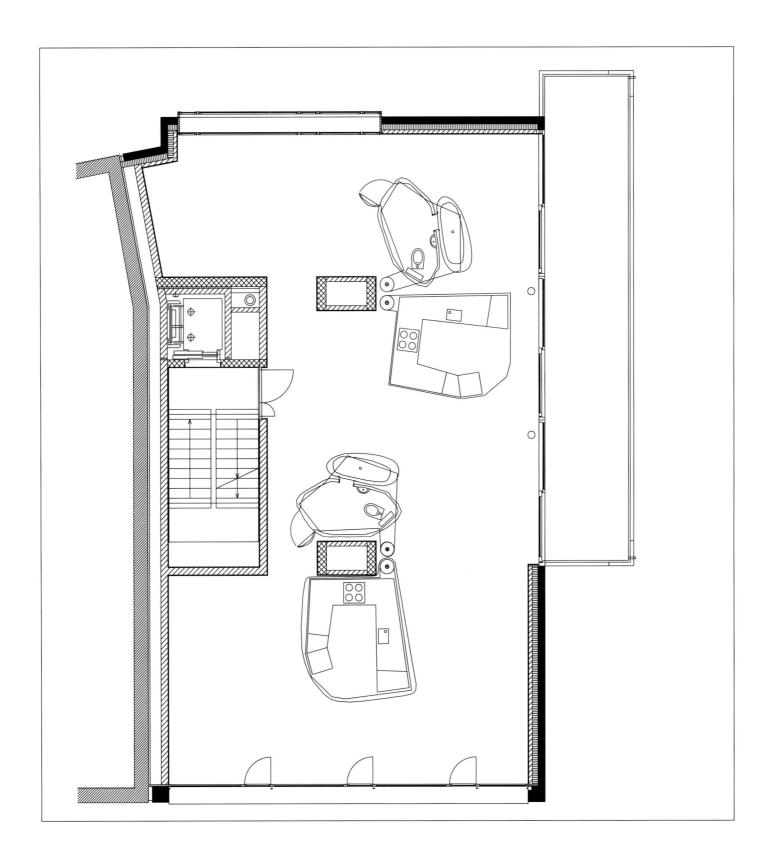

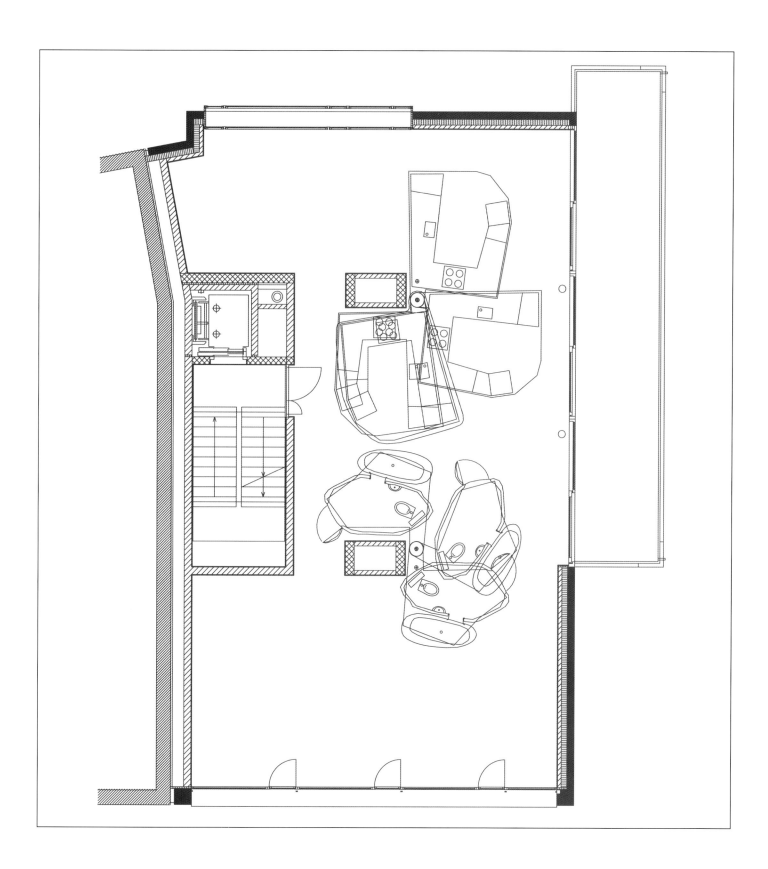

Dante Donegani / Giovanni Lauda
Jae-Kyu Lee, Elena Mattei

Photographs:
Roberto Baldessari

Disappearing Acts

Milan, Italy

Freeing up spaces is related to indulging in consumption.

One should concentrate the resources and functions to obtain greater domestic mobility and more liberty in the undesigned space.

By combining furniture and equipment and by using service-furniture, the home ought to be more autobiographical and free individual consumption from owning costly, definitive hardware.

Storage unit walls free the home's spaces. Domestic activities are enclosed inside pull-out components with standard dimensions : "custom made fully equipped boxes".

In this way empty space does not exclude a customer's pleasure.

The complexity and richness of the house finds a new temporary order. Furniture disappears, reduced to its "negative", moulds or cavaties shaped considering the forms of their inhabitants; or else they are integrated by electrical appliances in vanishing wall closets. Nature, boxed in and compacted (greenhouse, aviary, aquarium) becomes an environmental tent, an artificial landscape that mediates home and city.

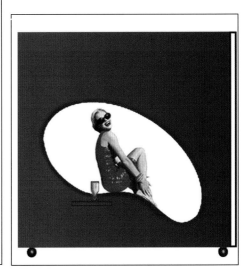

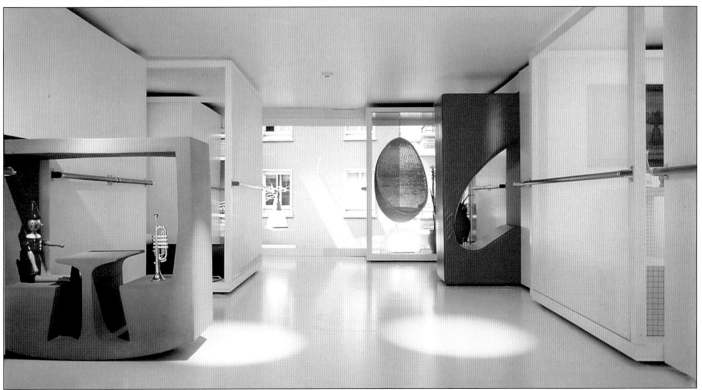

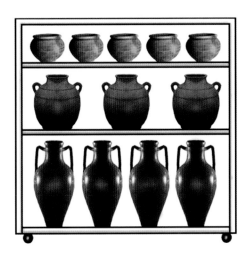

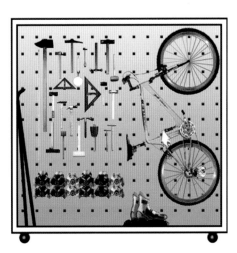

155

Allan Wexler

Photographs:
contributed by Allan Wexler

Vinyl Milford

Katonah, NY, USA

Vinyl Milford was commissioned by the Katonah Museum of Art. It explores the emotional and functional human needs that are crucial towards transforming a utilitarian shed into a home.

Vinyl Milford is the name of a mass-produced, vinyl coated sheet metal storage building manufactured by Arrow Industries. These storage sheds are fixtures of suburban American backyards, used to store lawn mowers and bicycles. They are inexpensive and practical stand-ins for the elegant out-buildings, guest houses and playhouses of country estates.

Vinyl Milford has been transformed into a complete guest house. Too small to contain a bedroom, bathroom, kitchen and dining room, the equipment and utensils needed for each of these functions bulge through the walls creating ghost-like forms of the furniture on the outside. As a function is required its equipment is pulled from the wall to inhabit the emptiness, defining the building for only one object and its activity. During the daytime the elements that constitute the bedroom are stored away in their sockets and the dining tables and chairs can slide into the room turning the entire house into a dining room. Vinyl Milford is totally empty when all the elements are stored away in the crate-like forms integrated into the exterior walls. The exterior walls show a sort of x-ray image of the various functions the interior can contain, all at once, defined by their characteristic artifacts.

Vinyl Milford is a suburban backyard survival kit, an anthropological investigation of our present lives. It presents everyday household objects as beautiful forms. The pillow, the flashlight, the water, the mirror are transformed into sculpture and their use into theater.

i-Box

Iwaoka, Myogo Pref, Japan

This small shed, which measures just 3 m × 3 m, was originally thought of as an object, like an oversized piece of furniture or a toy for children.

Construction was undertaken using materials which can be easily bought in a shopping center; steel pipes, rectangular pieces of lumber, sheets of plywood, plastic sheeting, screws, etc.

The design arose from some of the numerous drawings of "my dream house" painted by so many children of primary school age.

The structure of the box consists of 8 steel pipes for scaffolding, sandwiched between sheets of plywood inside and out.

These pipes are also used for the hinges of all of the doors and windows which open and close.

The construction of the box took the dedicated work of 5 people for 10 days, and half a day was required for dismantling.

An enormous number of children got into the box when it was used at a local summer festival in 2002 as the event's shop. After the summer festival, it was moved to the University campus for another festival in the autumn.

It is still being used at the present, having become a farmer's shed in the countryside, painted white and with a recently restored roof.

With one thing and another, the iBox has already undergone dismantling two times, but it has been constructed three.

163

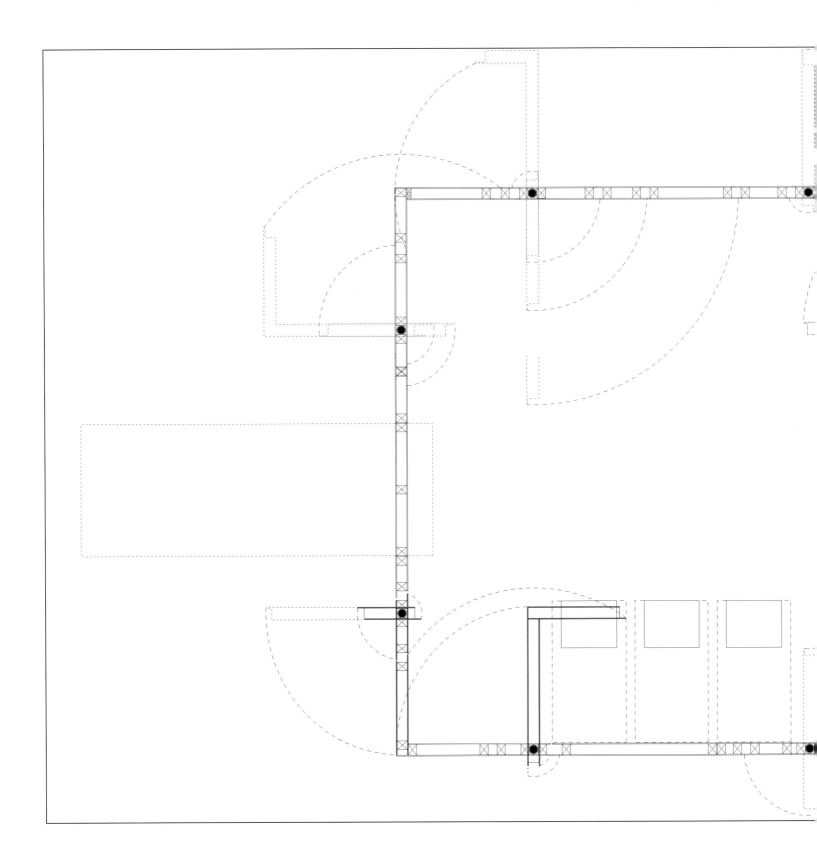

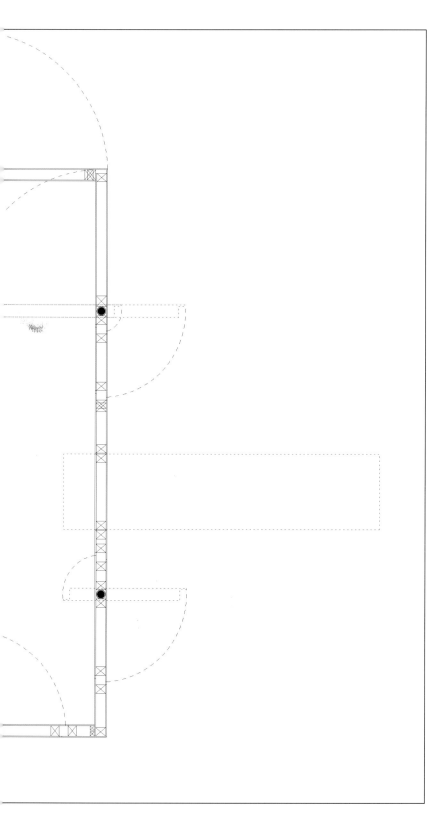

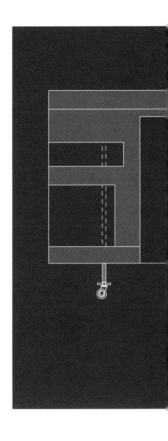

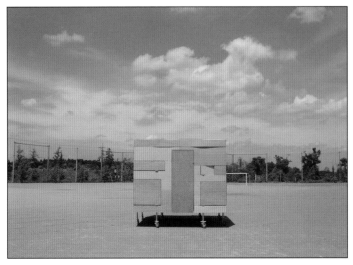

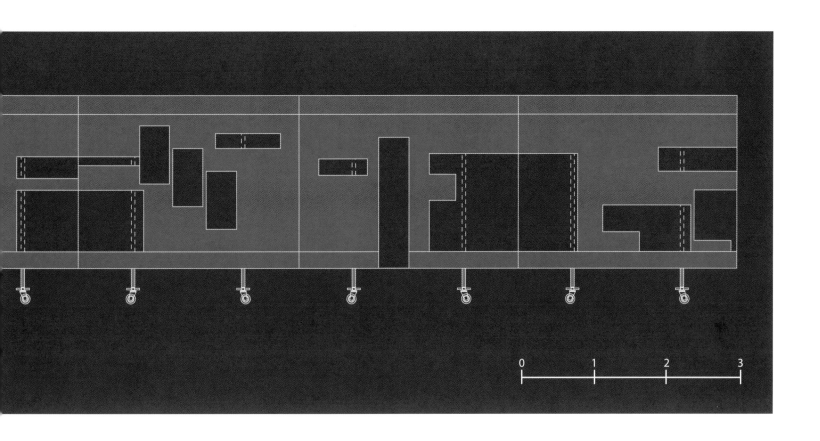

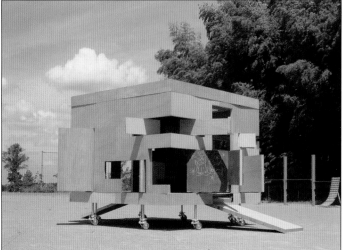

Kalhöfer - Korschildgen

Photographs:
Rolf Brunsendorf

Do It Yourself

Aachen, Germany

A terraced house in a housing estate from the 1920s changed hands and had to be adjusted to the requirements of the new owner. The original structure consisted of two levels with identical floor plans and the classic distribution: Kitchen, hall, bathroom, two rooms. By removing the partitions, the shell was reduced to its constructive minimum. The ground floor was opened up to create a large single space, open, bright, with no orientation to the street, the garden or the other rooms.

The spatial definition of this platform is left to the users. The subject of this design is not architecture but the aesthetics of use, it is a project to emancipate the client.

There are no fixed elements on the platform. Usually the kitchen is a very definite distribution item; here it can occupy optional positions and furniture can adjust to the new situation. Instead of a strict spatial sequence, a functionally and formally open system appears. The visitors' demands produce new combinations. Move the elements from the centre to the side and there will be enough room for dancing, working or just empty space – 'do it yourself'.

The industrial catering type kitchen entirely made of stainless steel was made to order for this project. The sinks are seamlessly stamped into the worktop. Heavy-duty rollers allow for easy rearrangement. The items are robust, matter of fact, and will soon be loaded with neutral looking crates, dustbins, utensils and electrical devices.

Service boxes, covered by colored and transparent industrial tarpaulins, offer connections (drainage, water supply, electricity) for the kitchen at three different locations. These transparent partitions are equipped with Velcro fasteners, which allow easy access to the installations. The industrial coupling devices make hooking up to the mains a simple operation. Light fittings are suspended from the ceiling to allow variable illumination. These tracks also supply electricity all along the worktop. If the distribution is changed, the supply sources can be rearranged as needed.

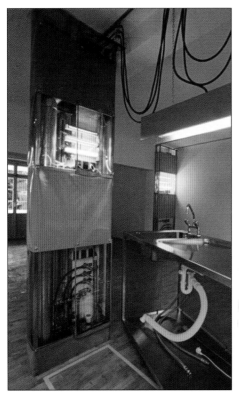

Horden, Cherry, Lee Architects,
Lydia Haack + John Höpfner Architekten

Micro Compact Home

Photographs:
Sascha Kletzsch,
T.U.M. Lehrstuhl Prof. Horden

O2 village, Munich, Germany

Inspired by the compact first-class airplane cabins, and the scale and order of a Japanese tea house, the 'Micro-Compact Home' is a lightweight, transportable and expandable living unit, measuring 8 ½ x 8 ½ feet (2.6 x 2.6 m) at a cost of 50.000 Euros. The tiny cube provides for working, dining for four, cooking, washing and sleeping in a double bed above. The kitchen bar serves both levels. The triple use lobby functions as bathroom and drying space for clothing. Storage is provided off each of the four spaces.

Basic modern facilities, energy outlets, water, etc. are foreseen. The modules are thermally insulated and comply with fire safety regulations. The materials are recyclable.

Alone or connected to others, the 'Micro Compact Home' provides valuable living space quickly and easily. The modular concept of minimized living units and urban alternatives facilitates the temporary use of land or spaces of different characteristics. By combining several 'micro compact homes' a small estate can appear, gradually completed with social spaces and other functions later. As requirements dictate the size, it develops to answer for the needs of daily life. The prefabricated modules can be delivered to the site by private car or a transport vehicle. Once there, a short time is sufficient to assemble a living space of the specified size.

Micro compact home ltd., in Austria, offers an outstanding product with comprehensive service from manufacture to delivery, with support in architecture, planning and interior design. m-ch can be delivered throughout Europe with project individual graphics and interior finishes.

Sponsored by the German mobile telephone company O2, the prototype entered production in June 2005. The project emerged from the group work at TUM (Munich Technical University). The first mini-estate for students is being constructed to the north of Munich. Its seven units were ready by October 2005.

© Technical Universitu of Munich, Lehrstuhl Prof. Horden

The drawings are copyright Haack + Höpnfner Architects

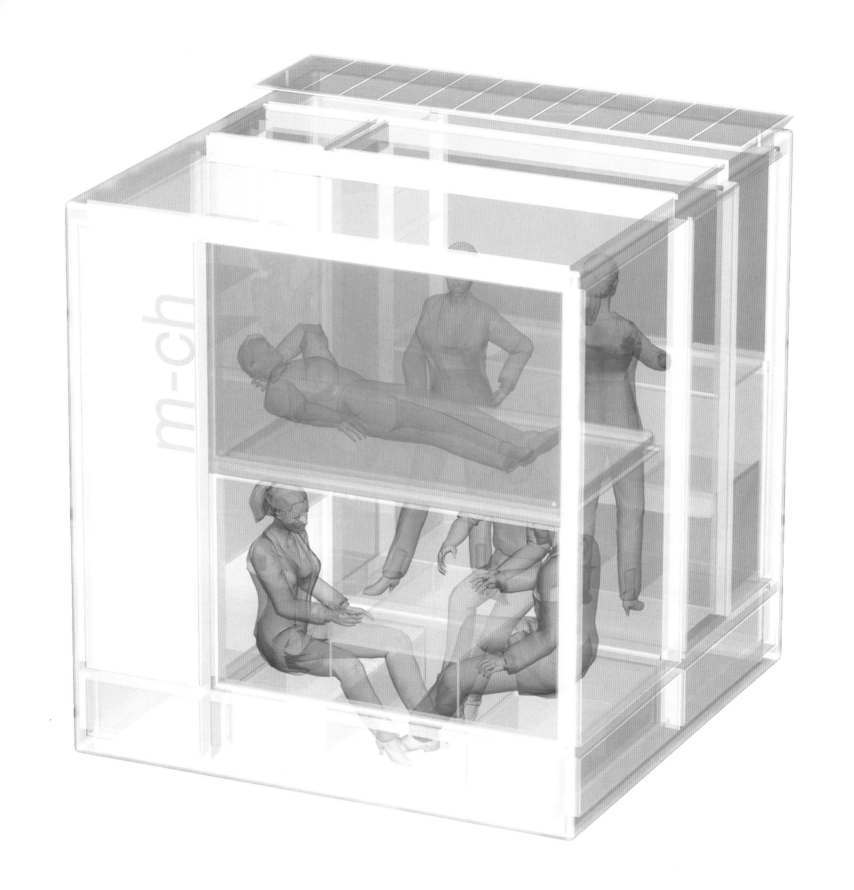

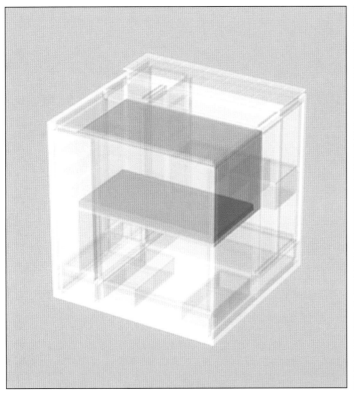
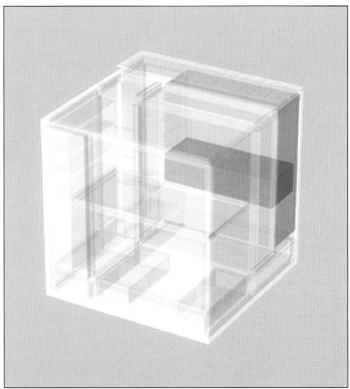
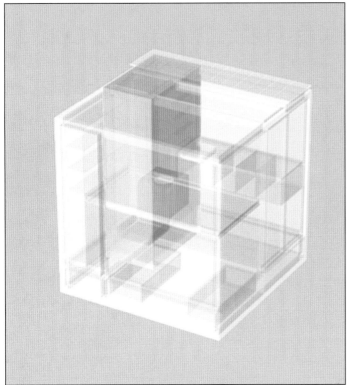
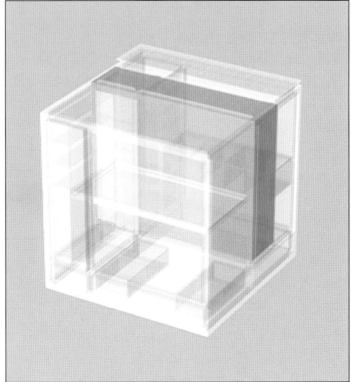

© Technical Universitu of Munich, Lehrstuhl Prof. Horden

176

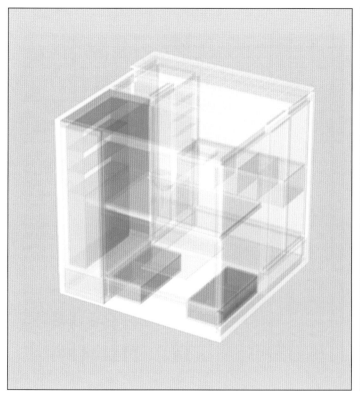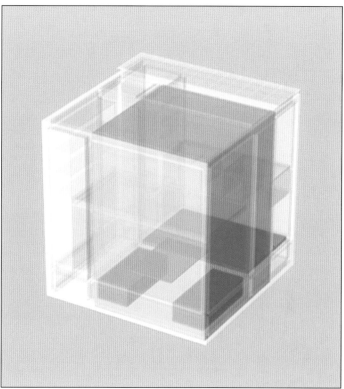

© Technical Universitu of Munich, Lehrstuhl Prof. Horden

© Technical Universitu of Munich, Lehrstuhl Prof. Horden

Alone or connected to others, the 'micro compact home' provides valuable living space quickly and easily. The modular concept of minimized living units and urban alternatives facilitates the temporary use of land or spaces of different characteristics. By combining several 'micro compact homes' a small estate can appear, gradually completed with social spaces and other functions later. As requirements dictate the size, it develops to answer for the needs of daily life. The prefabricated modules can be delivered to the site by private car or a transport vehicle. Once there, a short time is sufficient to assemble a living space of the specified size.

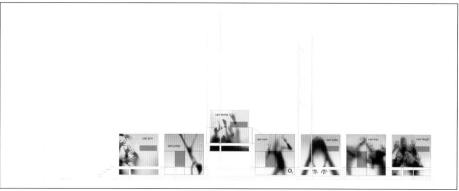

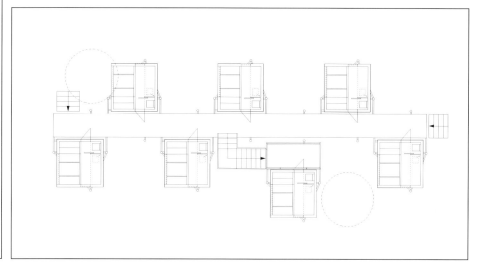

Stephanie Forsythe, Todd MacAllen

Photographs: contributed by the architects

Soft

Various locations

Molo's First Prize winning "softhouse" was installed in a former lodging house on the Bowery in New York, during the "First Step Open International Housing Competition 2003", sponsored by Common Ground. Expandable single occupancy rooms were placed within existing buildings as an experimental solution to homelessness. When not in use, the rooms can be squeezed back to free the common area.

Molo is a research oriented design studio formed in 2003 by Stephanie Forsythe, Todd MacAllen and Robert Pasut. "Softwall", already in production, is high up on Molo's list of innovative solutions to normal living problems.

Based on the ancient art of folding paper, "paper softwall" is an expandable partition designed for the ephemeral definition of separate spaces inside contemporary homes, offices or public areas. It can form a white, translucent wall, 12" thick (30cm). Originally 2" (5cm) thick when compressed, it can stretch to between 8' and 20' in length (2.5m-6m), 300 times its size. It dampens sound. It absorbs and transmits light. Made of recycled material, it is itself 100% recyclable. Felt ends with Velcro fasteners permit linkage of several walls in a series. Available heights range from 4' (1,2 m) to 12' (3 m). Softwall can be cut to size without specialized tools.

Other "soft" alternatives include:

"softsurface" can create apartition of almost any shape with a functional surface capable of bearing up to 10 lb weight if distributed on a tray.

"softlight", the moody ambient floor lamp made of flameproof paper was awarded first prize by International Lighting Design 2003.

"textile softwall" is like the paper version but made of a durable, tear resistant and water resistant, non-woven textile (a polyethylene based sheet material with "Class A" Flame Spread Rating, tending to shrink away from open flame).

Molo's soft items are part of New York MoMA's permanent collection.

The product's possibilities have been publicly demonstrated at several international events such as the "Design Beyond East and West" competition, hosted by Hanssem of Korea. A defining request was that entries should be installed within the limited floor plan of a typical Asian urban apartment. Softhouse was awarded the Golden Prize.

paper softwall

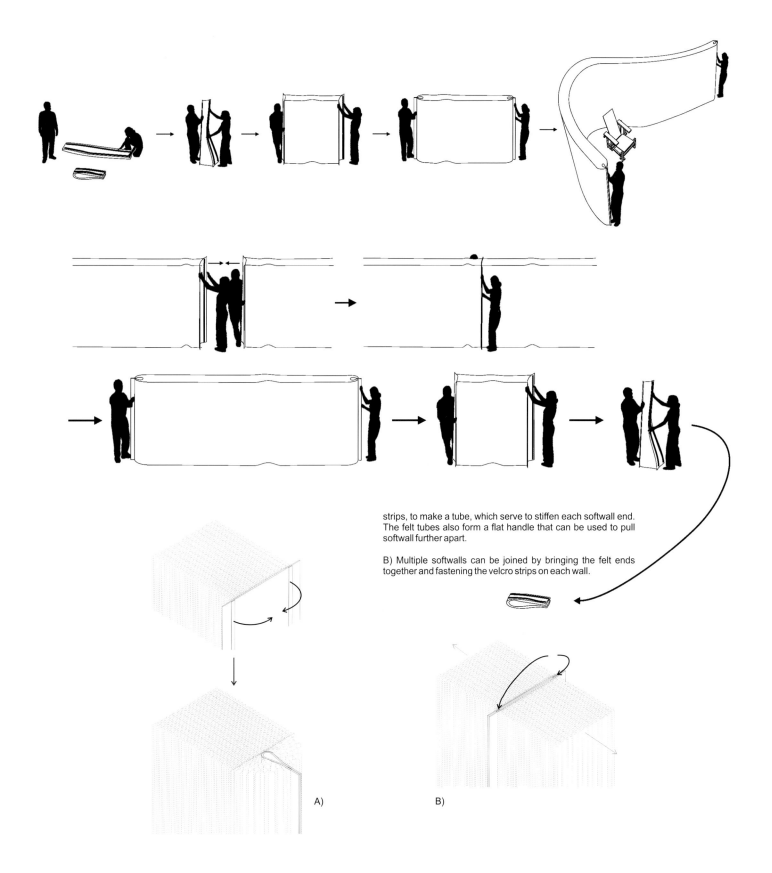

strips, to make a tube, which serve to stiffen each softwall end. The felt tubes also form a flat handle that can be used to pull softwall further apart.

B) Multiple softwalls can be joined by bringing the felt ends together and fastening the velcro strips on each wall.

A)

B)

textile softwall

softhouse

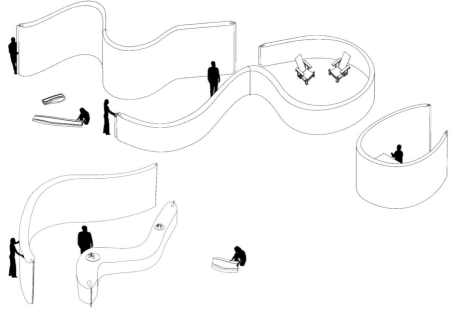

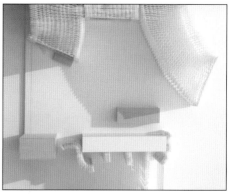

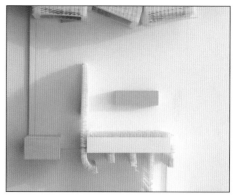

White Design

Photographs:
Bert Leandersson

Optibo

Göteborg, Sweden

Traditional living patterns are changing. Today 80% of Göteborg's population lives in one or two person households. Agenda 21, the sustainable development program adopted at the UN conference in Rio de Janeiro in 1992, calls for a 50% reduction of the environmental impact of building by the year 2021. In answer, the Optibo prototype explores the technical, environmental and human possibilities for future living and housing, by incorporating the functions of a 75 m^2 apartment into 25 m^2 without loss of living quality. The project is a joint venture by different business areas in property, technology, product and building sectors. Optibo is not compact living; it is plenty of room in a limited space: a large room with multiple usage options, instead of many small specialized subdivisions. At the control panel in the hall you can select a number of pre-programmed furniture layouts: much of the furniture has been multi-functionally designed and incorporated into the floor, under which there is a 60 cm space from which chairs, sofas, beds or tables emerge hydraulically to meet different demands. The table's height is variable, from dining to coffee to work station. In the various usage options the character of the flat can be altered by the lighting, for which fiber optics and LED lights have been chosen, with a lifetime of up to 20 years. The apartment's functions are regulated by computer technology. Heating and cooling are delivered automatically through newly developed gypsum panels in the ceiling, the venetian blinds close when the "bedroom" option is activated. At cleaning time, all the furniture disappears and the robotic vacuum cleaner comes out to do the work. The bathroom is accessible through a sliding frosted glass door. The materials and solutions chosen are environmentally sound, tested and used in new ways. Glass is used innovatively in walls, ceilings and kitchen design, combining warmth with a sensation of space. White Design believe the trend of socializing through cooking is set to continue, so a relatively large area in the flat is given to the well equipped kitchen. Naturally, containers for sorting at source are provided. The apartment is easy and cheap to maintain, and represents a contribution to environmental concerns and futuristic housing.

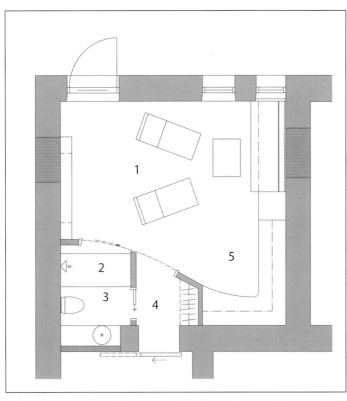

1. Dining room   3. WC   5. Kitchen
2. Bath   4. Hall

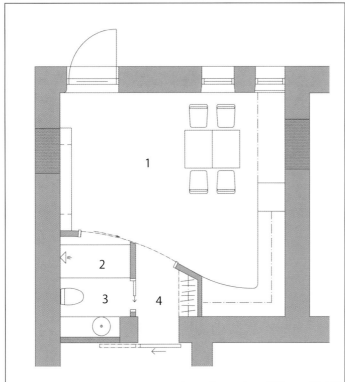

1. Living room   3. WC
2. Bath   4. Hall

| 1. Bedroom | 3. WC |
| 2. Bath | 4. Hall |

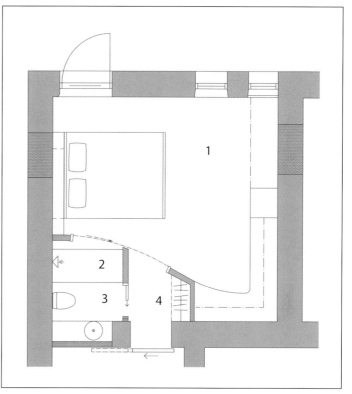

| 1. Workroom | 3. WC |
| 2. Bath | 4. Hall |

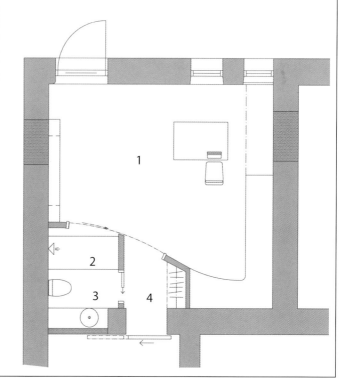

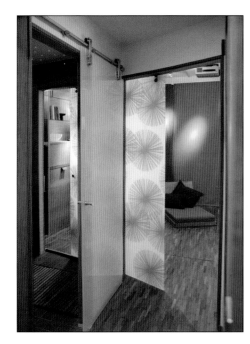

Drawer-House

Mejiro, Tokyo, Japan

The constant ebb and flow between action and rest, between a multifunctional cluttered space, and the restful reduction of a room's accessories to the minimum seems particularly relevant in city like Tokyo. The inspiration for Drawer House, as its name expresses, is the magic of concealing our plethora of miscellaneous objects behind closed screens or "drawers", keeping them for later. All the range of household functions – Tables, beds, shelves, partitions and whole rooms can be drawn out when they are wanted. The rest of the time, their existence can be temporarily forgotten. Basic functions, like the kitchen and the bathroom, are neatly hidden behind closed doors, Even the main access to the house or the openings onto the stairs are only signified by a discreet opening mechanism, so the home becomes a conjuring trick to which only the permanent inhabitants know the secret.

The building is distributed on three floors. The ground floor has a total surface area of 63.79m²; the first floor above is only 54.48 m², as it leaves some free space for a glass floor terrace. With 44.24 m², the basement is somewhat smaller still.

The site has been separated from the street by a fence of timber studs the whole height of the building. Sunshine filters through the studs and penetrates the almost entirely glass façade, shedding a stripy pattern of light on the slate floor downstairs; The opposite end of this room is brightly lit through the glass floor of the terrace upstairs. The walls and all the drawers and doors where all the accessories are waiting, are made of white ash plywood stained with natural white oil, throughout the house. The upstairs floor is oak. In the basement, the pale sandstone floor lightens a potentially oppressive space. The hidden interiors of all the drawers, such as bookshelves, beds, or other spaces, are finished in dark Japanese Liden plywood, starkly illustrating the opposition between visible and invisible.

The architects responsible for this solution pride themselves in their flexible approach to projects. The name of the firm, Nendo, means clay in Japanese. Oki Sato (of Nendo's seven-man design team), won the Good Design Award 2004.

Site plan

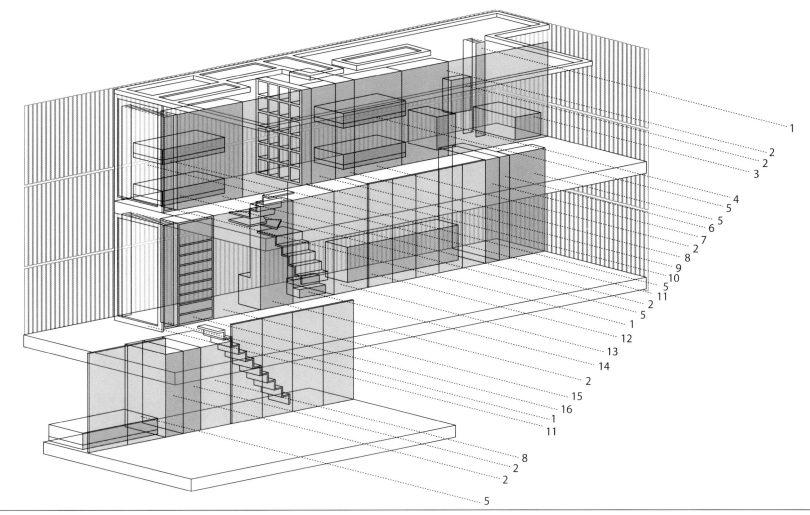

1. Curtain
2. Storage
3. Bath
4. Toilet
5. Bed
6. Cupboard
7. TV
8. Closet
9. Desk + chair
10. Bookshelf
11. Window
12. Kitchen
13. Lavatory
14. Stairs
15. Entrance
16. Cloak

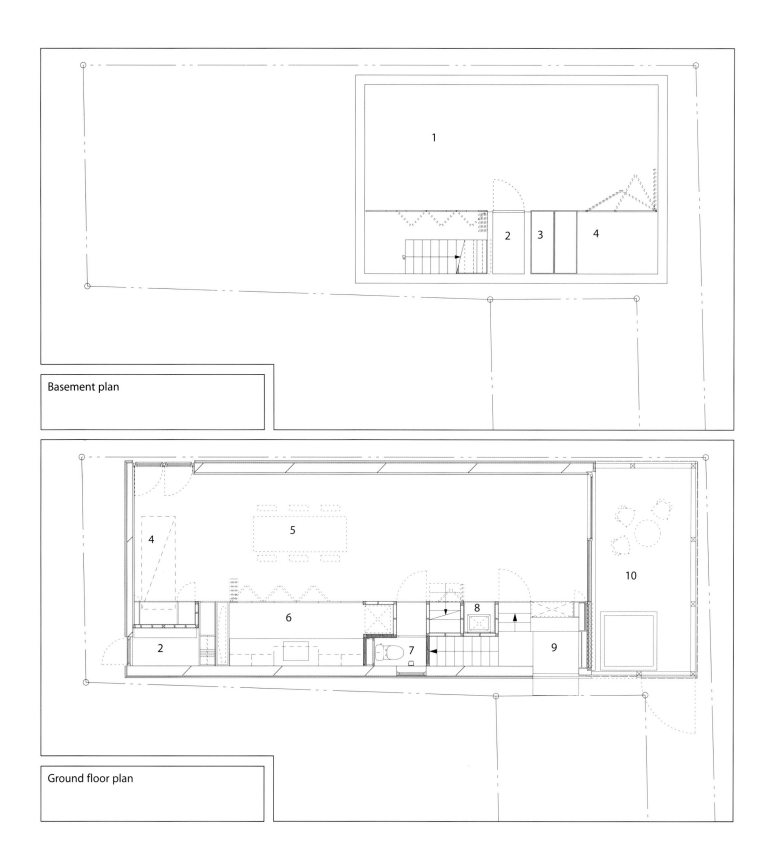

Basement plan

Ground floor plan

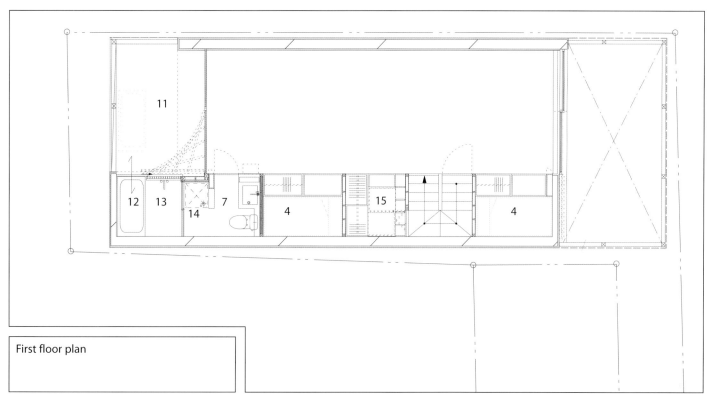

First floor plan

1. Audio room
2. Storage
3. Movable storage
4. Bed space
5. Dining
6. Kitchen
7. Toilet
8. Wash stand
9. Entrance
10. Balcony 1
11. Balcony 2
12. Bathtub
13. Bathroom
14. Washing machine
15. Closet/changing room

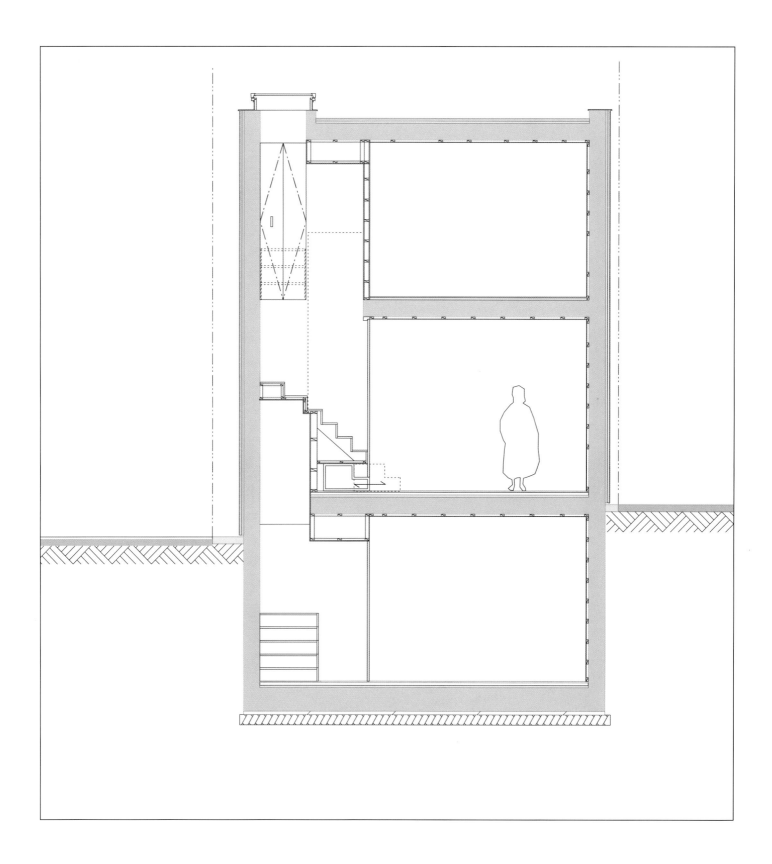